BURT NEUBORNE is an Associate Professor of Law at New York University Law School. An honors graduate of Harvard Law School, he has served as Staff Counsel to the New York Civil Liberties Union and as Assistant Legal Director of the American Civil Liberties Union. In addition to his extensive litigation in civil liberties, he has co-authored the Fourth Edition of POLITICAL AND CIVIL RIGHTS IN THE UNITED STATES and UNQUESTIONING OBEDIENCE TO THE PRESIDENT: THE A.C.L.U. CASE AGAINST THE VIETNAM WAR.

ARTHUR EISENBERG received his law degree from Cornell University, and has done graduate work in history at Columbia University and the London School of Economics. He is presently a Staff Counsel with the New York Civil Liberties Union where he has litigated extensively with Mr. Neuborne in the area of voting rights. Mr. Eisenberg lectures on civil liberties and constitutional law.

Also in this Series

AN AMERICAN
CIVIL LIBERTIES
UNION HANDBOOK

THE RIGHTS OF CANDIDATES AND VOTERS

THE BASIC ACLU GUIDE FOR VOTERS AND CANDIDATES

Burt Neuborne
Arthur Eisenberg

General Editors of this series:
Norman Dorsen, *General Counsel*
Aryeh Neier, *Executive Director*

 A DISCUS BOOK/PUBLISHED BY AVON BOOKS

78402

AVON BOOKS
A division of
The Hearst Corporation
959 Eighth Avenue
New York, New York 10019

Library of Congress Catalog Card Number: 76-15915

ISBN: 0-380-00626-X

First Discus Printing, June, 1976.

DISCUS TRADEMARK REG. U.S. PAT. OFF. AND
FOREIGN COUNTRIES, REGISTERED TRADEMARK—
MARCA REGISTRADA, HECHO EN CHICAGO, U.S.A.

Printed in the U.S.A.

Table of Contents

Preface

This guide sets forth your rights under present law and offers suggestions on how you can protect your rights. It is one of a series of handbooks published in cooperation with the American Civil Liberties Union on the rights of mental patients, prisoners, servicemen, teachers, students, women, suspects, gay people, hospital patients, and the poor. Additional books, now in preparation, will include volumes on the rights of the mentally retarded, children, aliens, civil servants, veterans, and the aged.

The hope surrounding these publications is that Americans informed of their rights will be encouraged to exercise them. Through their exercise, rights are given life. If they are rarely used, they may be forgotten and violations may become routine.

This guide offers no assurances that your rights will be respected. The laws may change and, in some of the subjects covered in these pages, they change quite rapidly. An effort has been made to note those parts of the law where movement is taking place but it is not always possible to predict accurately when the law *will* change.

Even if the laws remain the same, interpretations of them by courts and administrative officials often vary. In a federal system such as ours, there is a built-in problem of the differences between state and federal law, not to speak of the confusion of the differences from state to state. In addition, there are wide variations in the ways in which particular courts and administrative officials will interpret the same law at any given moment.

If you encounter what you consider to be a specific abuse of your rights you should seek legal assistance. There are a number of agencies that may help you, among them ACLU affiliate offices, but bear in mind that the ACLU is a limited-purpose organization. In many communities, there are federally funded legal service offices which provide assistance to poor persons who cannot afford the costs of legal representation. In general, the rights that the ACLU defends are freedom of inquiry and expression; due process of law; equal protection of the laws; and privacy. The authors in this series have discussed other rights in these books (even though they sometimes fall outside the ACLU's usual concern) in order to provide as much guidance as possible.

These books have been planned as guides for the people directly affected: therefore the question and answer format. In some of these areas there are more detailed works available for "experts." These guides seek to raise the largest issues and inform the non-specialist of the basic law on the subject. The authors of the books are themselves specialists who understand the need for information at "street level."

No attorney can be an expert in every part of the law. If you encounter a specific legal problem in an area discussed in one of these handbooks, show the book to your attorney. Of course, he will not be able to rely *exclusively* on the handbook to provide you with adequate representation. But if he hasn't had a great deal of experience in the specific area, the handbook can provide some helpful suggestions on how to proceed.

Norman Dorsen, General Counsel
American Civil Liberties Union

Aryeh Neier, Executive Director
American Civil Liberties Union

The principal purpose of these handbooks is to inform individuals of their rights. The authors from time to time suggest what the law should be. When this is done, the views expressed are not necessarily those of the American Civil Liberties Union.

Introduction

Long before there was a United States, there was an idea—an idea that political power emanated from the consent of the governed and that government should be an expression of popular will.

Long after the United States was formed, John Locke's idea remained just that—merely an idea. As recently as 1950, persons wishing to participate in the American political process were required to run a gauntlet of restrictions including poll taxes, literacy tests, residence requirements, and property ownership, which effectively disenfranchised millions upon millions of Americans.

The past 25 years have seen dramatic progress in removing the legal obstacles which impeded the realization of John Locke's idea. We have attempted to chronicle the broad outlines of that progress. In sketching the current state of our political rights, we have obviously not attempted a learned treatise. Instead, we have sought to present, in nontechnical form, the basic rights of persons seeking to vote or to run for office. Of

9

course, the proliferation of those rights cannot obscure the disquieting fact that even after 25 years of dramatic progress in removing legal obstacles to voting, only about one-half the qualified electorate actually votes. Clearly, reform of our archaic registration system and a more efficient administration of elections would raise the percentage to a more respectable level. The fact persists, however, that John Locke's vision of a state in which "the people shall be judge" has not yet been realized and, although we have reason to be proud of the accomplishments of the last quarter-century, we still have a long way to go before John Locke's idea becomes a reality.

BURT NEUBORNE
ARTHUR EISENBERG

I

The Role of the Courts and the Constitution in Protecting Voting Rights

Does the Constitution contain a clause protecting the right to vote and to run for office?

Not explicitly. For a society which is fond of regarding itself as the world's leading practitioner of democracy, our Constitution is guilty of an embarrassing lapse: it contains no broad guarantee of the right to participate in the democratic process. When the Constitution was adopted, the concept of universal suffrage was unthinkable. To most of the Founding Fathers, the franchise was a serious matter to be exercised only by responsible Caucasian males—preferably of property.[1] Indeed, the Constitution appears to have treated voting rights as a matter solely of state concern and permitted the states wide tolerance in deciding who could—and who could not—vote.[2] As political theory in America evolved toward a greater acceptance of universal suffrage, constitutional amendments guaranteed the vote to racial minorities, women and youths 18 to 21 years of age. However, in the absence of a general constitutional right to vote, courts prior to the

11

Warren era were unable—or unwilling—to fashion broad constitutional protection of voting rights.

Doesn't the provision in Article IV, Section 6 of the Constitution, which guarantees a republican form of government, protect the right to vote?

One would think so. However, since 1849, the Supreme Court has steadfastly refused to enforce the clause guaranteeing a republican form of government on the ground that it raises a "political question" beyond the competence of the judiciary.[3] Whether the Guarantee clause is any less susceptible to judicial enforcement than the even more amorphous Due Process or Equal Protection clauses is open to serious question. However, under current precedents, the Guarantee clause cannot be used to protect the right to participate in the democratic process.

What is a "political question" and why doesn't it completely bar the courts from dealing with voting rights?

The "political question" doctrine is designed to prevent the courts from deciding issues which should be decided only by the politically elected branches of government—Congress and the President. Thus, the political question doctrine has precluded courts from passing on issues of foreign policy (such as the recognition of foreign governments); military training and preparedness (such as the appropriate methods of training the Ohio National Guard in the aftermath of Kent State); the legality of the Vietnam war, and the "republican" nature of states seeking entry into the Union. Unfortunately, through a semantic misunderstanding, several courts confused the political question doctrine with a ban on deciding all cases affecting political rights. However, the Supreme Court has repeatedly repudiated such a misguided view of the political question doctrine and it is now clear that it does not bar courts from protecting voting and other "political" rights.[4]

Why doesn't the First Amendment's protection of freedom of speech also guarantee the right to vote and to run for office?

Courts could have viewed the act of voting as the quintessential exercise of free expression in a democracy and protected voting rights by assimilating them into the First Amendment, much as associational rights were engrafted onto a First Amendment which did not expressly protect them.[5] Unfortunately, however, while overtones of First Amendment protection occasionally appear in Supreme Court opinions,[6] most courts have not viewed voting and related political rights as protected by the First Amendment, except in an occasional rhetorical flourish.

How did the Warren Court find constitutional protection for voting rights?

Prior to the 1960's, no body of Supreme Court precedent existed which gave protection to the general right to vote. However, the Warren Court borrowed a legal principle which had been forged in the 1940's to protect leafleters and street-corner orators from discriminatory treatment and utilized it as an effective doctrinal handle to safeguard the right to vote. In order to control the grant of permits, the Supreme Court ruled in the 1940's that if a permit was granted to one group to engage in speechmaking, leafleting or parading, local officials could not lawfully deny other groups a similar permit.[7] This principle, which came to be known as the "equal access" principle, was seized upon by the Warren court to protect the right to participate in the democratic process. Just as a permit to use a publicly owned auditorium for a lecture could not be granted to one group but denied to another, so, the Warren Court reasoned, the "permit" to participate in the democratic process could not be selectively distributed without a showing of overriding governmental interest. Thus, whenever a state "permitted" some people to vote, but denied the vote to others, state officials were obliged to justify the disparate treatment—just as if they had treated two groups differently when each sought permits to leaflet in the park.[8]

How did the Warren Court describe the newly evolved doctrine protecting voting rights?

Traditionally, the "equal access" principle has been expressed by the Supreme Court in its most obvious doctrinal manifestation—the constitutional command that no person be denied the equal protection of the laws. Accordingly, when the Warren court imported the equal access principle into the voting area, it naturally phrased its decisions in the comfortable vernacular of the equal protection clause. Unfortunately, by casting its voting decisions in an equal protection mold, the Warren court inadvertently linked judicial protection of the franchise to an unstable and highly controversial jurisprudence.

Why does the Equal Protection Clause provide less than satisfactory protection of the Right of Franchise?

While the rise of the Equal Protection Clause as a device to protect voting rights was an enormous improvement on the past judicial failure to afford any broad constitutional protection to the right to vote, it has one serious drawback: the lack of a consensus view as to the appropriate standard of judicial review.

Traditionally, statutes reviewed under the Equal Protection Clause were sustained so long as the reviewing court could imagine a rational basis for the distinction at issue. Thus, so long as a statute advanced a legitimate governmental interest and so long as its distinctions bore a rational relationship to the advancement of the legitimate interest, a challenged statute would be upheld. Such a permissive standard would rarely, if ever, invalidate a statute, and if it were applied to most statutes restricting the right to vote, the statute would be almost automatically upheld.

In order to avoid the results of the permissive "rational relationship" test, the Warren court evolved a "new" Equal Protection test whenever a "fundamental" right such as voting was at issue. Under the "new" test, the governmental interest did not merely have to be "legitimate"; it had to be "compelling." Moreover, the distinctions at issue did not have to be merely "rationally related" to the governmental interest; they had to be "necessary" for its attainment. If the interest could be advanced by "less drastic means," the statute was unconstitutional. Such "strict scrutiny" virtually doomed any voting restriction which came before it.[9]

All would have been well had the Warren court majority remained intact. However, the erosion of the Warren court's majority endangered the neat two-tier system of Equal Protection review which had flourished from 1969 to 1972. Moreover, even apart from the erosion of the Warren court's majority, concerned jurists expressed uneasiness with a doctrine which forced a reviewing court to choose between two extreme standards of review: one of which virtually ensured the validation of the statute and one which virtually ensured its demise. Various experiments with tests lying somewhere between the extremes were launched, and the area continues to be beset with confusion and controversy.

What test does the current Supreme Court use to review statutes restrictive of the Franchise?

Reflecting the controversy and uncertainty which surrounds Equal Protection jurisprudence, the current

Court has not evolved a uniform approach to voting cases. The Warren Court holdovers—Justices Brennan and Marshall—faithfully apply the "compelling state interest advanced by the least drastic means" test and, predictably, vote to invalidate almost all restrictions on voting and candidacy.[10] Justice Powell, reflecting the concern for voting rights exhibited in his later years by his predecessor, Justice Harlan, has, more often than not, applied the strict scrutiny test.[11] On the other hand, Justices Rehnquist and Blackmun, occasionally joined by Chief Justice Burger, have urged abandonment of the Warren court's strict scrutiny test and urged a return to the permissive "rational relationship" test.[12] Justice Stewart, who expressed initial reservations about utilizing the equal access principle as a substitute for a general guarantee of the right to vote, applies the Warren court test to those statutes which absolutely bar a person from voting, but applies a more permissive standard to statutes merely rendering it difficult to vote.[13] Justice White, occasionally joined by the Chief Justice, appears to apply a test less stringent than the "strict scrutiny" test, but more exacting than the "rational relationship" standard of review.[14] The net result is a shifting coalition of Justices giving little or no guidance to the lower courts.

Is there a way out of the Equal Protection tangle?

The area might become clearer if the Court recognized that the initial purpose of the equal access principle when it was established in the 1940's was the protection of First Amendment activity. It is precisely because participation in the democratic process is so closely bound up with the First Amendment that the Warren court so naturally applied "equal access" to protect the franchise in the 1960's. Perhaps the time has come to abandon the veneer of Equal Protection which the Warren court utilized and recognize that voting and running for office are First Amendment rights. Until such a hidden First Amendment component is accepted, however, voting rights law will remain a creature of the Equal Protection Clause and will be very much subject to its vagaries.

NOTES

1. Thomas Emerson, David Haber, and Norman Dorsen, *Political and Civil Rights in the United States,* 4th ed. by Norman Dorsen, Paul Bender and Burt Neuborne (Boston: Little, Brown & Co., 1976) Vol. I, p. 848. Chapter XIII of *Political and Civil Rights* contains an intensive discussion of the legal authorities which govern the rights discussed in this book.
2. E.g. Pope v. Williams, 193 U.S. 621 (1904) (upholding durational residence requirements for voting). For the modern view of residence requirements for voting, see *infra,* Chapter 3.
3. E.g. Luther v. Borden, 48 U.S. (7 How.) 1 (1849); Baker v. Carr, 369 U.S. 186 (1962).
4. E.g. Baker v. Carr, 369 U.S. 186 (1962).
5. NAACP v. Alabama, 357 U.S. 449 (1958).
6. Williams v. Rhodes, 393 U.S. 23, 41 (1968) (Justice Harlan, concurring); Kusper v. Pontikes, 414 U.S. 51 (1973).
7. For a modern application of the principle, see Chicago Police Dep't. v. Mosley, 408 U.S. 92 (1972).
8. The first case which explicitly applied the equal access principle to voting restrictions was Kramer v. Union Free School District, 395 U.S. 621 (1969).
9. The apogee of the strict scrutiny test occurred in Dunn v. Blumstein, 405 U.S. 330 (1972).
10. E.g. O'Brien v. Skinner, 414 U.S. 524, 531 (1974) (Justices Marshall, Douglas, and Brennan concurring).
11. E.g. Rosario v. Rockefeller, 410 U.S. 752, 763 (1973) (Justice Powell, dissenting).
12. E.g. O'Brien v. Skinner, 414 U.S. 524, 535 (1974) Justices Blackmun and Rehnquist, dissenting). But

see Justice Blackmun's "liberal" vote in Hill v. Stone, 421 U.S. 289 (1975).

13. Compare Kusper v. Pontikes, 414 U.S. 51 (1973) with Rosario v. Rockefeller, 410 U.S. 752 (1973) and Justice Stewart's "conservative" vote in Hill v. Stone, 421 U.S. 289 (1975).

14. Phoenix v. Kolodziejski, 399 U.S. 204 (1970). See also Justice White's "liberal" vote in Hill v. Stone, *supra*.

II

The Right to Vote

A common tenet of the American democratic ideology has been that universal suffrage is intrinsic and fundamental to the nation's political system. But when it has come to expanding the franchise and providing for universal suffrage, each generation's definition of the universe has been different and, in some significant respects, limited. Indeed, throughout the American political experience, universal suffrage has been more honored in the breach than in the observance. From the earliest colonial period to the present, varying kinds of voter qualification requirements have been imposed which have effectively narrowed the universe of eligible voters.

The right to vote in early colonial settlements was typically dependent upon ownership of property. But, as colonial America became more complex and as it moved toward revolution, attitudes regarding the franchise began to change. The prevalent democratic ideology of the revolution and then of the post-revolutionary period, while not fully accepting of universal suffrage, could not tolerate the continued limitation of the suffrage only to the propertied class. The post-revolutionary period, in particular, witnessed wide-spread redrafting of constitutions by the former colonial commonwealths and the initial drafting of constitutions by newly created states. A hallmark of these new constitutions was the abandonment of the property qualifications for voting. But, with the elimination of the property requirements, new forms of voter qualifications were thought necessary to insure a responsible electorate. Thus, in instances where property qualifications were abandoned, the states often substituted the requirement that the franchise be limited instead to taxpayers. Similarly, laws for the first time began to allow only citizens to vote. The Ohio constitution of 1803, a document that was widely imitated by the Western states, introduced the requirement that a potential voter must live in a community for at least a year before such person could vote in that community. This sort of qualification, which became known as a durational residency requirement, was generally followed in other states. Moreover, throughout this early period of the Republic, scant recognition was given to the electoral rights of women, of non-whites, and of persons below the age of twenty-one. Consequently, by the mid-nineteenth century, although property requirements were eliminated in virtually all states, the percentage of popular participation in the franchise did not increase substantially beyond the electoral involvement of the colonial period. Suffrage was typically limited to a very narrow universe composed of white taxpaying male adults above the age of twenty-one.[1]

The expansion of that universe, particularly with regard to women and blacks, was a painful and arduous struggle that extended from the mid-nineteenth century well into the mid-twentieth century. The beginning of an organized women's suffrage movement is commonly perceived as dating back to the Seneca Falls Convention in 1848. Yet it was not until August 1920 that the Nineteenth Amendment was ratified, thereby conferring upon women the equal right to vote. The black struggle for equal voting opportunities has, if anything, been even more frustrating and difficult. Prior to the Civil War, all but five states barred non-whites from the franchise. This injustice was only partially rectified when, in 1870, the Fifteenth Amendment was ratified and states were, thereafter, prohibited from abridging the right to vote "on account of race, color, or previous condition of servitude." Unfortunately, the Fifteenth Amendment did not end racial discrimination at the polling places. Instead it caused such discrimination to be accomplished by more subtle devices as well as by some very unsubtle extralegal methods. Beginning with the end of the Reconstruction period in the middle 1870's, blacks living in the South were increasingly denied the vote by conduct ranging from bureaucratic caprice to more severe acts of individual harassment and intimidation. By the end of the nineteenth century, however, a variety of more sophisticated legal devices such as "grandfather clauses," "poll taxes," "literacy requirements," and "white primaries" were introduced with the design of disenfranchising the black man. The degree to which such devices succeeded in effecting the desired exclusion is dramatically demonstrated by the following figures: In 1867, 66.9 percent of the black male voting population in Mississippi registered to vote. In that same year, 55.0 percent of the white male voting age population in Mississippi was registered. In 1892, 5.7 percent of the eligible black population registered, while 56.5 percent of the white eligible population was registered. A similar pattern prevailed in Louisiana where in 1896, 130,334 blacks were registered to vote but, in 1904, following the introduction of literacy, property, and poll-tax qualifications, only

1,342 were registered. These racially discriminatory devices persisted well into the mid-twentieth century when a variety of federal laws and constitutional provisions were enacted, nearly one hundred years after the ratification of the Fifteenth Amendment, in an attempt to finally fulfill the promise of that earlier Amendment.[1]

Today, although the vestiges of the poll taxes have been consigned to constitutional oblivion and although property and sex qualifications and durational residency requirements may no longer be enforced, the goal of massive, universal participation in the electoral process remains elusive. The major contemporary impediments to widespread voter participation, however, are onerous registration procedures and archaic voting practices which continue to limit the franchise in many states to the better educated and politically sophisticated members of the electorate. Voter registration laws were initially instituted in the late nineteenth century as progressive reforms. At the time of their introduction, the registration schemes were justified as advancing the dual interests of minimizing electoral fraud and insuring an interested and concerned electorate. But, the widespread adoption of voter registration laws has had an astonishing result. Between 1864 and 1910, before voter registration laws were introduced, approximately 76.8 percent of the eligible voters participated in presidential elections. During the period after 1900 when voter registration schemes were widely implemented, only about 59 percent of the eligible electorate voted in presidential elections. Thus, despite strenuous legislative and judicial efforts in recent years to expand the universality of electoral participation, current voter involvement remains at a disturbingly low level and severely skewed in favor of the better educated groups in society.[2]

How far has the American polity advanced in realizing the ideal of universal suffrage? As this chapter demonstrates, the gains have been substantial. But, as the dreary election statistics also demonstrate, only about one-half of the eligible electorate participates in American politics. Until substantial segments of the submerged, inactive constituents are encouraged to engage in electoral politics, neither participatory democracy nor universal suffrage will have been realized.

How old must you be to vote?

The Twenty-sixth Amendment establishes a uniform voting age in all state and Federal elections of not more than 18 years of age. If a voter will have reached 18 on or before election day, he or she may register to vote, even though he or she is not yet 18 on registration day. However, even if voters will be 18 by the time the general election is held, they cannot vote in a primary until they actually turn 18.[3] States or local governments may further lower the voting age below 18 if they wish. Many communities permit persons under 18 to vote in certain elections. Congress, if it wished, could lower the voting age by statute to below 18 for Federal elections. However, Congress lacks the power to force states and localities to further lower the voting age in state and local elections.[4] Finally, the Twenty-sixth Amendment has been held inapplicable to Indian tribal elections in which the age qualification varies from tribe to tribe.

Can the right to vote be conditioned upon the ability to read, write or understand the English language?

No. The Federal Voting Rights Act Amendments of 1970 suspended the use of literacy tests in Federal, state, and local elections and this statutory prohibition against literacy tests was recently extended, at least through 1982, by the 1975 Federal Voting Rights Act. The Supreme Court has upheld Congress's power to suspend all literacy tests, in local as well as Federal elections.[5]

Thus, the present prohibition on literacy tests is based on the Voting Rights Act and is not based upon any constitutional requirement. In 1959, prior to the enactment of the Voting Rights Act, Virginia's literacy requirement was unanimously upheld by the Supreme Court, although more recent cases suggest that a literacy test might be unconstitutional as well as a violation of the Voting Rights Act.[6]

Do election officials have an affirmative obligation to assist illiterates and voters who cannot read or understand English?

Yes. The 1975 amendments to the Voting Rights Act provide significant protection to members of language minorities and require bilingual elections whenever 5 percent of the eligible voters in a locality are members of a language minority. Even before the adoption of the 1975 Act (discussed in Chapter VI), several courts imposed affirmative constitutional obligations on election officials to assist illiterates and persons who do not read or understand English by posting interpreters at the polls, providing bilingual ballots, and assisting in the marking of ballots.[7] If official assistance is offered to illiterate voters, election officials may bar private persons from rendering assistance. If, however, certain handicapped voters are permitted private assistance, similar assistance may not be denied to illiterates.[8]

Can the right to vote be conditioned upon the payment of a poll tax?

No. In 1964, with the ratification of the Twenty-fourth Amendment, the use of the poll tax in federal elections was prohibited. Nevertheless, subsequent to the ratification of the Twenty-fourth Amendment, poll taxes continued to be imposed at the state and local level in four states.[9] Finally, in 1966, in *Harper* v. *Virginia State Board of Elections*,[10] the Supreme Court declared poll taxes unconstitutional; concluding that "a State violates the Equal Protection Clause of the Fourteenth Amendment whenever it makes the affluence of the voter or payment of any fee an electoral standard."

Can the right to vote be conditioned upon the ownership of property, or on the payment of taxes?

No. As a general proposition, the right to vote cannot be conditioned upon the ownership of property or upon the payment of taxes.

In declaring poll taxes unconstitutional in 1966, in *Harper* v. *Board of Elections,* the Supreme Court expressed hostility to laws that conditioned the franchise upon wealth. Nevertheless, the precise question of the constitutionality of a statute that limited the franchise to property owners was not confronted by the Court until 1969. In that year, in *Kramer* v. *Union Free School District No. 15*,[11] the Court invalidated a New York statute that permitted only persons who either leased or owned taxable property or persons who were parents of school-age children to vote in school-board elections.

On the same day as the *Kramer* decision the Supreme Court also decided *Cipriano* v. *City of Houma*,[12] involving a Louisiana statute that gave only "property taxpayers" the right to vote in special elections called to approve the issuance of revenue bonds by municipally owned public utilities. In a unanimous decision, the Supreme Court held such a property qualification unconstitutional. Again, in *Phoenix* v. *Kolodziejski*,[13] the Supreme Court invalidated an attempt to restrict the franchise in general revenue bond elections to property owners.

Finally, in *Hill* v. *Stone*,[14] the Supreme Court extended the *Kramer, Cipriano,* and *Phoenix* line of cases to invalidate a requirement that voters tender some real personal property, no matter how small, for taxation prior to voting in municipal revenue bond elections. After *Hill* v. *Stone,* election officials may not impose a property qualification test on prospective voters in any general election.

May ownership of property ever be required in order to vote in an election?

Yes. In 1973 a divided Supreme Court recognized a narrow class of elections which may be restricted to property owners. If an electoral district exists to advance a narrowly limited purpose and if its decisions disproportionately affect property owners, the Supreme Court has upheld a requirement that restricted the vote to affected property owners.[15] Thus, while property qualifications may not be required in municipal bond or school-board elections, the franchise in certain water irrigation district elections may be restricted to the owners of the benefited property. Obviously, the line between a "limited purpose" election which disproportionately affects property owners and a general election is difficult to draw. Thus far, school-board elections and virtually all municipal bond referenda have been held to constitute general elections. Thus, under current guidelines, only extremely rare situations would justify the imposition of a property requirement for voting.

How long must a person have lived in a community in order to be permitted to vote?

The requirement that an individual be obliged to live in the community for a period prior to being permitted to vote is called a "durational residency" requirement. Prior to 1972, states and localities routinely required persons to have lived in the community for periods ranging from 90 days to one year prior to permitting them to vote. However, in 1972, in *Dunn* v. *Blumstein*,[16] the Supreme Court declared all durational residence requirements for voting unconstitutional. Thus, the theoretical answer to the question is that the length of a person's prior residence in the community is irrelevant to voting. However, as a practical matter, Justice Marshall recognized in *Dunn* that because of clerical necessity, registration rolls must close a reasonable period prior to an election—a period which Justice Marshall suggested should not exceed 30 days. Since any person moving into the community after registration for an election has closed would be ineligible to vote, the "clerical necessity" period imposes a short *de facto* residence requirement. Subsequently, the Supreme Court upheld the closing of registration rolls for state and local elections up to 50 days before the election.[17] Thus, as a practical matter, if you move into a community less than 50 days before an election, you may be prevented from voting in it; although most states adhere to Justice Marshall's admonition that registration rolls should not close earlier than 30 days before the election.

In the case of presidential elections local officials must, pursuant to the Voting Rights Act, keep registration rolls continuously open until 30 days before the election.[18] Thus, if you move into a community at least 30 days prior to a presidential election, you must be permitted to register and to vote in it, even if local registration has already closed. Moreover, even if you move in after registration for the presidential election has closed, you must be permitted to vote for President by absentee ballot from your prior residence.

In summary, in state, local and congressional elections, while 50 days is the longest you can be required to have lived in the community prior to voting, 30 days is the maximum period most communities require. Many communities require even less. For presidential elections, 30 days is the longest you can be required to have lived in the community prior to voting and even if you are banned under the 30-day test, you can vote by absentee ballot from your prior residence.

Of course, if you move into a community but fail to register, you will not be permitted to vote even if you have resided in the community for substantial periods of time. Limitations on onerous registration practices are discussed *infra*.

Can the franchise be limited to persons who are good-faith residents of the communities in which they seek to vote?

Good-faith residence, for voting purposes, is most frequently equated with the legal definition of "domicile." While the precise definition of "domicile" may vary somewhat from state to state, as a general proposition, "domicile" is defined as a fixed place of habitation accompanied by an intention to remain at that place either permanently or indefinitely.

Legal disputes involving the good-faith residence of persons seeking to vote arise most significantly in the context of particular classes of persons, such as servicemen, university students, and hospital patients, who are regarded as too transient to be permitted to vote by and in the communities in which they live.

The theoretical justification for denying transients the right to vote in local communities is their insufficient interest in the local elections. But, in many instances, the actual reason underlying resistance to the local enfranchisement of such persons is their power as a substantial voting bloc with concerns and interests that are often different from and antithetical to the rest of the community.

Where may servicemen vote?

Prior to 1965, many jurisdictions forbade servicemen stationed within their borders from acquiring a voting residence so long as they remained on active duty. The antiservicemen rules were justified as necessary to protect against callous voting by transients and to prevent base commanders from exerting undue influence over local affairs. In *Carrington* v. *Rash*,[19] however, the Supreme Court invalidated Texas' absolute bar against servicemen voting, ruling that if a serviceman satisfied the traditional tests for acquiring a voting residence in Texas—physical presence plus an intention to remain for the foreseeable future—his status as a serviceman could not prevent him from acquiring a voting residence. Thus, under current law, members of the armed forces may acquire a voting residence at their duty stations so long as they intend to remain there for the foreseeable future. Alternatively, members of the armed forces may cast absentee ballots from the homes to which they intend to return after their period of service has ended. Federal law provides for convenient and expeditious absentee balloting for servicemen.

Where may residents of Federal enclaves vote?

Residents of Federal enclaves—such as the National Institute of Health—may acquire a voting residence in the state which surrounds the enclave. Prior to 1970, many jurisdictions argued that the relatively short stay of persons residing in Federal enclaves precluded them from acquiring a voting residence in the surrounding localities. However, in *Evans* v. *Cornman*,[20] the Supreme Court ruled that residents at the National Institute of Health were sufficiently affected by the laws and practices of Maryland to require Maryland to permit them to acquire a Maryland voting residence.

Where may college students vote?

Prior to the ratification of the Twenty-sixth Amendment, the appropriate voting residence of college students was rarely contested. However, with the voting age lowered to 18, college communities have waged, with mixed results, a vigorous rear-guard action to force college students to vote by absentee ballot from their parents' homes. Several jurisdictions erected irrebuttable presumptions against students' acquiring a voting residence. Just as similar antiservicemen restrictions were invalidated by the Supreme Court, antistudent regulations which absolutely forbid student voting have been universally invalidated.[21] Several jurisdictions sought to avoid student voting by presuming that students were residents of their parents' community unless they could prove otherwise. Such "rebuttable presumptions" against student voting have generally, although not invariably, been invalidated.[22] Finally, the most sophisticated antistudent provisions have taken the form of so-called "neutral" statutes which single students out for special scrutiny to determine the true "locus of their primary concerns," without establishing any presumption concerning voting residence. While many courts have refused to tolerate subjecting student residence claims to more searching inquiry than would be applied to the public at large,[23] a disturbing number of courts have upheld the practice.[24] Although such a scheme appears facially valid, it delegates to often hostile local officials the task of determining the *true* "locus of a students' primary concerns." Not surprisingly, local officials, under such a scheme, more often than not find students' voting residence to be elsewhere.

Two initial objections to student voting have been decisively rejected. First, the mere fact of dormitory residence does not preclude the acquisition of a voting residence and, second, an intent to leave the college community upon graduation does not preclude the acquisition of voting residence. However, students asserting a voting residence in their college community may be required to submit objective evidence to buttress their contention that it is the "locus of their primary concerns." Among the potentially significant factors which are often weighed are location of bank accounts; automobile registration; motor vehicle license address; and income tax returns.[25]

May Americans residing abroad establish a voting residence in local, state, or national elections?

Until very recently, Americans residing abroad were not permitted to vote in state, local, or national elections. Since the right to vote in national, state, and local elections was entirely dependent upon establishing a voting residence in some state, many persons residing abroad failed to satisfy state or local requirements regarding actual residence. Consequently, even though such persons remained United States citizens, remained subject to the draft and continued to pay taxes, they were barred from voting even in presidential elections because they possessed no residence within the United States. Although several jurisdictions were quite liberal in permitting Americans living abroad to retain an address from which they might register and vote by absentee ballot, in the absence of such a second home, many Americans residing abroad were disenfranchised. In 1976, Congress enacted legislation guaranteeing the right to vote in presidential elections to expatriate Americans in the state of their last American residence. Americans residing abroad continue to be barred from voting for members of Congress and state and local officials.[26]

Can persons who have been convicted of felonies be deprived of the right to vote?

Yes. In most states, persons who have been convicted of felonies are excluded from the franchise. The underlying rationale for excluding such persons is not entirely clear. It is clear, however, that such exclusionary provisions were common to the earliest state constitutions that were adopted in eighteenth and nineteenth-century America. And it is therefore evident that such provisions can be traced to an era when participation in the franchise was perceived as a privilege to be exercised only by a discrete class composed of propertied white males.

But, apart from an appreciation of the historical antecedents of these provisions, any effort to understand the contemporary justifications for the exclusion of former felons reveals a variety of amorphous concerns, no one of which seems compelling. Throughout the judicial opinions that seek to uphold such disenfranchisement provisions, there are vague allusions to a legislative interest in protecting the "purity of the ballot box." This interest is occasionally described, somewhat differently, as a concern that persons whose antisocial behavior has been demonstrated and proved should not be permitted to participate in important societal functions like the franchise. On other occasions, an even more theoretical justification is advanced in support of such exclusionary provisions which derives from Locke's concept of the "social contract." As articulated by Judge Friendly of the United States Court of Appeals for the Second Circuit, this rationale rests upon the perception that a person who has broken the law and violated an element of the "social contract" has thereby abandoned the right to participate in further administering the compact.[27] The most straightforward explanation of such provisions, however, is that they are penal in nature and that the deprivation of the franchise is yet another form of punishment that is imposed upon persons convicted of felonies.

In reality, any reasoned retention by the states of these ex-felon disenfranchisement provisions is dependent upon some combination of all the foregoing justifications. Nevertheless, because no single justification had seemed persuasive and because, in recent years, laws restricting the franchise have undergone serious judicial review, provisions that affected the disenfranchisement of ex-felons had seemed particularly vulnerable to legal invalidation. And within the past few years an increasing number of judicial challenges to such provisions had been undertaken. However, in *Richardson* v. *Ramirez* [28] the Supreme Court upheld those provisions of a California law that disenfranchised ex-felons. In the *Ramirez* case, the Court reasoned that the California law could not be said to violate the Equal Protection Clause because Section 2 of the Fourteenth Amendment specifically allows the disenfranchisement of persons "for participation in rebellion, or other crime."

May voters be compelled to register before being allowed to vote?

Virtually every American jurisdiction requires eligible voters to register prior to the election in order to be permitted to vote. While the constitutionality of voter registration statutes has never been before the Supreme Court, the widespread belief that registration is necessary to prevent fraud virtually guarantees broad approval of such statutes.

The American voter registration system is unique in Western democratic practice. Registration of eligible voters in every other democracy is viewed as a responsibility of government—similar to Selective Service and census taking. In the United States, however, the inertial burden of discovering when and how to register is placed on the prospective voter. Moreover, many

American jurisdictions administer archaic and cumbersome registration rules which render it extremely difficult to register. Not surprisingly, therefore, many observers view outdated registration practices as the single largest impediment to increasing participation in the electoral process. New York has recently enacted the nation's first mail registration statute, and similar proposals are pending in Congress.[29]

The courts have placed minimal restrictions on the registration process. In *Beare* v. *Smith* [30] a Texas registration scheme which required annual reregistration at least 8 months before an election was invalidated as too restrictive. The closing of registration rolls 50 days before an election has been sustained.[31] In presidential years, however, registration must be kept continuously available up to 30 days before the election. Courts have not yet begun to explore the legal implications of geographically inaccessible registration centers and registration hours.

Does a voter have the right to vote by absentee ballot?

Most jurisdictions provide absentee ballots for persons who are unable to be present at the polls. In *O'Brien* v. *Skinner*,[32] the Supreme Court ruled that New York's refusal to permit pretrial detainees confined within their county of residence to vote by absentee ballot while permitting detainees confined outside their counties of residence to vote by absentee ballot was unconstitutional. Whether *O'Brien* signals the emergence of a general constitutional right to an absentee ballot is doubtful. The 1970 amendments to the Voting Rights Act provide for convenient and uniform absentee balloting in presidential elections. The failure of several states to provide absentee ballots for primaries has been upheld.[33]

Does the right to vote include the right to vote in a primary or sign a nominating petition?

Yes. Despite some initial waffling, the Supreme Court has repeatedly ruled that the right to participate in the nominating process is an integral part of the right to vote. Thus, a refusal to permit a voter to participate in a primary or to sign a nominating petition is subject to the same level of judicial scrutiny as an outright denial of the right to vote in the general election. Of course, the special nature of a primary as the expression of the desires of a political association may impose special qualification requirements. For example, a primary may be restricted to duly enrolled party members. Moreover, the Supreme Court has ruled that states may require that persons have been members of the party for a reasonable period of time prior to voting in the primary in order to protect against bad-faith raiding. In *Rosario* v. *Rockefeller*,[34] New York's requirement that a prospective primary voter have enrolled in the party prior to the last preceding general election (8 to 11 months prior to the primary) was narrowly upheld. However, in *Kusper* v. *Pontikes*,[35] similar Illinois requirements of a 23-month party membership prior to primary voting or signing a nominating petition were invalidated. Special problems of intraparty regulations are discussed *infra*.

NOTES

1. For general chronologies of the franchise see Williamson, *American Suffrage; From Property to Democracy* (1960) and Porter, *A History of Suffrage in the United States* (1918). For an account of the women's suffrage movement see Flexner, *Century of Struggle* (1959). Discussions of the impact of the "Black Codes" are presented in United States Commission on Civil Rights, *Political Participation* (1968) and Wood-

ward, *Origins of the New South,* 321–349 (1951).
It was not until 1915, and again in 1939, that the
Supreme Court invalidated racial grandfather clauses
in the voting area as a violation of the Fifteenth
Amendment. Guinn v. United States, 238 U.S. 347
(1915); Lane v. Wilson, 307 U.S. 268 (1939). White
primaries survived until 1944 and 1953. Smith v. Allwright, 321 U.S. 649 (1944); Terry v. Adams, 345
U.S. 461 (1953). Poll taxes were not invalidated until
1966. Harper v. Virginia Board of Elections, 383 U.S.
663 (1966). Literacy tests were not suspended until
the passage of the Voting Rights Act of 1965.
Women did not receive the vote nationally until 1920.
Many property qualifications for voting survived and,
despite judicial hostility, continue to generate litigation. Hill v. Stone, 421 U.S. 289 (1975). Durational
residence requirements were not invalidated until
1972. Dunn v. Blumstein, 405 U.S. 330 (1972). The
voting age was not lowered to 18 until 1971.

2. Discussions of the impact of voter registration laws
    on electoral participation are presented in Kelley,
    Ayres & Bowen, *Registration and Voting: Putting
    First Things First,* 61 Am. Pol. Sci. Rev. 359 (1967)
    and Comment, *Access to Voter Registration,* 9 Harv.
    Civil Rights & Civil Liberties Law Rev. 482 (1974).

3. Gaunt v. Brown, 341 F. Supp. 1187 (S.D. Ohio 1972).

4. Oregon v. Mitchell, 400 U.S. 112 (1970).

5. Oregon v. Mitchell, *supra.*

6. Lassiter v. Northampton County Board of Elections,
    360 U.S. 45 (1959). See also, Cardona v. Power, 384
    U.S. 672 (1966).

7. E.g. Puerto Rican Organization for Political Action v.
    Kusper, 350 F. Supp. 606 (N.D. Ill. 1972) aff'd. 490
    F. 2d 575 (7th Cir. 1973) (bilingual assistance);
    Garza v. Smith, 320 F. Supp. 131 (W.D. Tex. 1970)
    vacated for entry of fresh decree, 401 U.S. 1006,
    app. dism. 450 F. 2d 790 (5th Cir. 1971) (illiterates).

8. Cf. James v. Humphreys County Board of Elections,
    384 F. Supp. 114 (N.D. Miss. 1974) with Smith v.
    Arkansas, 385 F. Supp. 703 (E.D. Ark. 1974).

9. Alabama, Mississippi, Texas, and Virginia.

10. 383 U.S. 663 (1966).

11. 395 U.S. 621 (1969).
12. 395 U.S. 701 (1969).
13. 399 U.S. 204 (1970).
14. 421 U.S. 289 (1975).
15. Salyer Land Co. v. Tulare Lake Basin Water Storage Co. 410 U.S. 719 (1973).
16. 405 U.S. 330 (1972).
17. Marston v. Lewis, 410 U.S. 679 (1973); Burns v. Fortson, 410 U.S. 686 (1973).
18. Bishop v. Lomenzo, 350 F. Supp. 576 (E.D.N.Y. 1972.)
19. 380 U.S. 89 (1965).
20. 398 U.S. 419 (1970).
21. E.g. Jolicoeur v. Mihaly, 5 Cal. 3d. 565, 488 P. 2d 1, 96 Cal. Rptr. 697 (1971).
22. E.g. Whatley v. Clark, 482 F. 2d. 1230 (5th Cir. 1973).
23. E.g. Frazier v. Callicutt, 383 F. Supp. 15 (N.D. Miss. 1974).
24. Ramey v. Rockefeller, 348 F. Supp. 780 (E.D.N.Y. 1972); Ballas v. Symm, 494 F. 2d 1167 (5th Cir. 1974).
25. Ramey v. Rockefeller, *supra.*
26. The electoral plight of expatriate Americans is discussed in Hardy v. Lomenzo, 349 F. Supp. 617 (S.D. N.Y. 1972). See, Overseas Voter Act of 1976, 42 U.S.C. 1973.
27. See Green v. Board of Elections, 380 F. 2d 445 (2nd Cir. 1967).
28. 418 U.S. 24 (1974).
29. McKinney's Election Law, §153
30. 321 F. Supp. 1100 (S.D. Tex. 1971) aff'd sub. nom. Beare v. Brisco, 498 F. 2d 244 (5th Cir. 1974).
31. See note 12, *supra.*
32. 414 U.S. 524 (1974).
33. Fidell v. Board of Elections, 343 F. Supp. 913 (E.D. N.Y. 1972) aff'd 409 U.S. 972 (1972).
34. 410 U.S. 752 (1973).
35. 414 U.S. 51 (1973).

III

The Right to Run for Office

The threshold qualifications that persons seeking to run for office must satisfy are quite similar to those which are generally imposed upon persons seeking to vote and which were discussed in the preceding chapter. In virtually all states prospective candidates must, at a minimum, qualify as registered voters. Frequently, however, additional qualifications such as durational residency or increased age requirements are imposed upon prospective candidates.

Can minimum age requirements be imposed upon persons seeking to run for office?

Yes. It is common for states to require that candidates for significant electoral office be of a minimum age. The minimum age requirements imposed upon candidates are often more restrictive than those imposed generally upon persons seeking to vote. Litigation challenging such requirements has been almost entirely unsuccessful.[1]

Federal constitutional challenges to minimum age

38

requirements were severely undercut by the observation
that the Federal Constitution itself requires that members of the House of Representatives be at least 25
years old, that senators be at least 30, and that the
president have attained the age of 35.

**Can candidates be required to own property as a
precondition to running for office?**

In virtually all elections, property qualifications for
candidates would be unconstitutional. The leading case
is *Turner* v. *Fouche*,[2] where the Supreme Court invalidated a Georgia law that limited school-board
membership to the owners of real property. After not-
ing that the Georgia law would allow a person owning
"a single square inch of land" to qualify as a school-
board member, the Supreme Court concluded that the
law advanced no rational state interest. The Court
disdained the suggestion that a citizen who was in all
other respects qualified to be a school-board member
could be assured of rendering responsible decisions
regarding the educational process only if that person
were also the owner of real property.

In *Turner,* the Supreme Court found the law in
question to be so irrational that it invalidated the Georgia provision by utilizing the traditional "rational basis"
test. Consequently, the Court found it unnecessary to
reach the question of whether property qualifications
for candidates should be measured against the more
rigorous requirements of the "compelling state interest"
test. But other courts have invoked the "compelling
state interest" test to invalidate property qualification
laws using a variety of legal theories to justify the
invocation of strict judicial scrutiny. Several courts,
including the New York Court of Appeals,[3] have
viewed property qualification laws as a form of discrimination based upon wealth and have for this reason
subjected the laws to strict scrutiny. Other courts have

invoked the "compelling state interest" test on the theory that the right to run for office is a fundamental personal right and that any substantial abridgment of that right must be measured against the requirements of the compelling state interest test. Still other courts have urged that property qualifications for candidates also abridge the fundamental rights of persons who wish to vote for candidates who might not satisfy the property qualifications, and for that reason, such qualifications must be subjected to strict judicial scrutiny.

There is, however, some suggestion that under very limited circumstances property qualifications might be upheld. In two cases decided by the Supreme Court in its 1973–1974 term, property qualifications for voting in so-called "special purpose" elections were upheld. Presumably, such requirements if legitimately applicable to voters could also be equally applied to candidates.[4]

Can candidates be required to pay a fee in order to run for office?

Not if they cannot afford it. The Supreme Court has ruled that candidate filing fees may not be constitutionally applied to prevent poor candidates from running for office. In *Lubin* v. *Panish,*[5] a Texas candidate filing fee system was deemed unconstitutional as applied to indigent candidates. However, several courts have refused to invalidate filing fees when the complaining candidate was financially able to pay them or when an alternative method of obtaining ballot status existed.[6] A discussion of regulations governing the appearance of candidates on the ballot appears *infra.*

Can potential candidates be required to live in the community for a minimum period of time before they can run for office?

While durational residence requirements have been

invalidated for voters, reasonable durational residence requirements are probably constitutional for candidates. In *Sunnunu* v. *Stark, Kanapaux* v. *Ellisor,* and *Chimento* v. *Stark,* lower Federal courts have recently upheld the constitutionality of New Hampshire's 7-year residence requirement for governor and state senator and South Carolina's 5-year residence requirement for governor.[7] Since the Supreme Court did not issue an opinion, a number of questions remain unresolved. First, what is the maximum durational period which will be permitted; second, may durational residence requirements be imposed on candidates for Federal, rather than state, office and, finally, may localities impose intrastate durational requirements in order to run for local office? Many courts have invalidated local—as opposed to state—residence requirements and the law in the area remains uncertain, with a substantial body of authority both upholding and invalidating local durational requirements.[8]

Can candidates be required to file loyalty oaths?

Prior to having their names appear on the ballots, candidates and political parties are often required by statute to file what are commonly described as "loyalty oaths." The constitutionality of such loyalty oaths depends upon the form and manner in which such oaths are worded. In some instances, the oaths require the candidates and parties to affirm that they will support the constitutions and laws of the state and Federal governments. Such oaths have been held to be valid provided they are carefully drafted and limited to an affirmation that the particular officeholder will engage in conduct supportive of or, alternatively, will not engage in conduct intentionally destructive of, the presently constituted system of government. But in some instances, the oaths require that potential candidates disclaim an intent to *advocate* the alteration or even the overthrow of the constitutional form of government. For example, an Indiana law required that in order for any party to appear on the ballot, the party must file a sworn statement, declaring that it does not "advocate the overthrow of local, state or national government by force or violence." The constitutionality of this law was tested when, during the 1972 presidential election, it was used to bar the Communist Party of Indiana from access to the ballot. The court test ultimately reached the United States Supreme Court and in the 1974 decision of *Communist Party* v. *Whitcomb,* the Court invalidated the Indiana loyalty oath provision.[9]

In some instances, loyalty oath provisions assume a different form. Instead of requiring candidates and parties to affirm personal or organizational support for the present system of government, some states specifically exclude certain parties from the ballot on the theory that the parties so excluded are endemically subversive. Thus, for example, the Communist party is specifically excluded from the ballot in many jurisdictions. Other states allow their state attorney general to designate certain parties as subversive and to thereby exclude such parties from the ballot. Such laws that exclude specific political parties from the ballot would appear to be unconstitutional for a number of reasons. The most obvious reason is that "such exclusion effectively punishes party members on the basis of their political beliefs" and therefore unconstitutionally abridges the rights of speech, conscience, and association which are protected by the First Amendment. But, a second and somewhat more subtle reason has been suggested for holding such exclusion to be unconstitutional. This second reason is based upon the following analysis: a legislative finding that certain parties are subversive is tantamount to a legislative finding of guilt. Accordingly, the statutory exclusion of certain parties from the ballot based upon the legislative finding of guilt is an unconstitutional bill of attainder.

In sum, only those loyalty oath provisions whose focus is carefully limited to knowingly illegal conduct can be regarded as even arguably valid.

Must a candidate be a member of a political party in order to seek its nomination?

Political parties may, if they wish, refuse to permit nonmembers to seek party nomination. For example, New York requires a prospective nominee to be an enrolled party member, unless the party leadership permits "outsiders" to enter the primary. In many states, persons who have been members of an opposing party may not seek the nomination of a new party for several years. The purpose of such laws is to prevent bad-faith changing of parties in order to weaken or wrest control of a rival party. Thus, Ohio refuses to permit a person to seek the nomination of a political party if he or she has voted in the primary of an opposing party during the preceding 4 years.[10] California imposes a similar 17-month waiting period before a party-switcher may seek nomination of a new party.[11] Restrictions on party candidacy are discussed more fully in Chapter VIII, *infra*.

Do the courts apply the same tests in reviewing restrictions on candidacy as they do in reviewing restrictions on voting?

Many persons have argued that restrictions on potential candidates are as serious an interference with constitutional rights as are restrictions on voting. Certainly the holdovers from the Warren court apply the same test to both and will uphold a restriction on either voting or candidacy only if it advances a compelling governmental interest by the least drastic means. However, a majority of the current Supreme Court appears to apply a more permissive test to candidacy restrictions than to laws restricting the right to vote. Thus, durational residency tests for voting have been invalidated, while even longer residence requirements for candidacy have been sustained; poll taxes and other financial impediments to voting have been absolutely banned, but candidate filing fees have been banned only if the particular candidate cannot pay; restrictions on party-switching by voters have been severely limited by the Court; while even more onerous restrictions on party-switching by candidates have been sustained; onerous clerical and registration requirements for voting have been invalidated, while onerous petition requirements for candidates have been sustained. Thus, although significant judicial protection exists for persons seeking to run for office, courts appear to tolerate a greater degree of state interference with the right to run for office than with the right to vote.

NOTES

1. E.g. Manson v. Edwards, 482 F. 2d. 1076 (6th Cir. 1973).
2. 396 U.S. 346 (1970).
3. Landes v. Town of North Hempstead, 20 N.Y. 2d 417, 231 N.E.2d. 120, 284 NYS2d 441 (1967).
4. The "special purpose" exceptions are discussed *supra.*
5. 415 U.S. 709 (1974).
6. Adams v. Askew, 511F. 2d 700 (1975); Matthews v. Little, 498 F. 2d. 1068 (5th Cir. 1974); Cassidy v. Willis, 323 A2d 598 (Del. 1974) aff'd 419 U.S. 1042 (1974).
7. Sunnunu v. Stark, 383 F. Supp. 1287 (D.N.H. 1974); Kanapaux v. Ellisor, ——— F. Supp. ——— (D.S. Car. 1974) aff'd 419 U.S. 891 (1974); Chimento v. Stark, 353 F. Supp. 1211 (D.N.H. 1973) aff'd. 414 U.S. 802 (1973).
8. Green v. McKeon, 468 F. 2d 883 (6th Cir. 1972);

Headlee v. Franklin County Board of Elections, 368 F. Supp. 999 (S.D. Ohio 1973).

9. 414 U.S. 441 (1974).
10. Lippitt v. Cipollone, 405 U.S. 1032 (1972).
11. Storer v. Brown, 415 U.S. 724 (1974).

IV

Access to the Ballot

The secret ballot in its contemporary form has not
been a constant feature of the American electoral system. While many early American communities utilized
written ballots, in a great many other communities the
vote was taken either by a public shows of hands or
by a voice vote, commonly called the *viva voce* method.
Indeed, the practice of public voting persisted in Missouri until 1863, in Virginia until 1867, and in Ken-
tucky until 1890. The formalities of this practice have
been described in the following manner:

> . . . [V]oting was done openly or viva voce, as it
> was called, and not by ballot. The election judges,
> who were magistrates, sat upon a bench with their
> clerks before them. Where practicable, it was cus-
> tomary for the candidates to be present in per-
> son, and to occupy a seat at the side of the judges.
> As the voter appeared, his name was called out
> in a loud voice. The judges inquired, "John Jones
> (or Smith), for whom do you vote?"—for gover-

nor, or whatever was the office to be filled. He replied by proclaiming the name of his favorite. Then the clerks enrolled the vote, and the judges announced it as enrolled. The representative of the candidate for whom he voted arose, bowed, and thanked him aloud; and his partisans often applauded.[1]

The virtues of public voting were that it fostered individual accountability and responsibility in the exercise of the franchise. Its deficiencies were that it invited intimidation, reprisals, and retaliation against persons for the way they voted. As the nation grew in population, and became so urbanized and impersonal a society that the constraints of public accountability were increasingly less effective, the inadequacies of public voting procedures were perceived to outweigh their advantages. Consequently, by the middle of the nineteenth century, most states adopted electoral procedures involving the use of a written ballot.

Still, the ballot procedures that were used in the nineteenth century were in several respects quite different from the practices that prevail today. The typical nineteenth-century ballots were not official ballots prepared and printed by the government. Rather, the ballots were printed by the individual candidates who ran for office or by the political parties that sponsored the candidates. Accordingly, the ballots did not contain the names of all of the candidates for office, but only those candidates who were supported by the particular party that had printed the ballot. Each party's ballot was distinguished by a different color or by some other identifying feature, and the ballots were distributed by the parties and candidates in advance of the elections. On election day the voter would go to the polling place and deposit the ticket of his choice in the ballot box.

The system of unofficial ballots proved susceptible of abuse and vulnerable to fraudulent practices. Under this system, the secrecy of the ballot was never assured because the distinguishing colors and characteristics of each party's ballot made it possible for partisans situated at the polling place to detect the candidate or party for which a voter had cast his vote. The distribution of ballots in advance of the elections also enabled voters to deposit more than one ballot in the box by folding one ballot inside another. Moreover, the unofficial ballot system allowed rival political parties to counterfeit their adversaries' ballots in such a way as to omit certain names from the counterfeited ballot and thereby deceive the unwary voter. The variety of fraudulent practices that resulted from the unofficial ballot system precipitated an increased demand for electoral reform which ultimately led to the adoption at the close of the nineteenth century of the "Australian" ballot system.

The Australian ballot, which derived its name from its country of origin, was characterized by the following features: the ballot was an official ballot which was prepared and printed by the government at public expense; it contained the names of all the candidates who were duly nominated; it was distributed at the polls and completed in a secret polling booth and then deposited in the ballot box. By 1900 a majority of the states adopted the Australian ballot, and by 1950 its use prevailed throughout the entire country.

The widespread adoption of the Australian ballot system created new problems. Since under the Australian system, ballots were officially prepared by election administrators, questions arose regarding the arrangement of names on the ballot and the criteria for determining whose names should appear on the ballot. The question of ballot arrangement was ultimately resolved in most states by adopting one of two approaches. In approximately thirty states, a party-column ballot was developed in which all of the nominees of each party were grouped together in one vertical column. Most of the remaining states adopted an office-block ballot which was organized so that all of the nominees for each office were grouped together.

The more difficult issue has involved the criteria for determining the persons whose names should appear on the official ballot. The use of an official ballot necessitated the further enactment of laws that would enable the preparers of the ballot to determine which candidates were the legitimate nominees of the parties; which organizations could legitimately qualify as political parties; and whether and how candidates not affiliated with parties could qualify for access to the ballot. Such laws which regularized the nominating process had the effect of excluding certain persons—particularly minority parties and independent candidates—from the ballot. The exclusion was further exacerbated by the demands of the progressive and other municipal reformers for a shorter ballot.

The demand for a short ballot was based upon the claim that the electorate was becoming confused by ballots which contained too many candidates and too many issues. Consequently, such progressive reformers as Herbert Croly argued that the short ballot would "concentrate the attention of the electorate on the selection of a much smaller number of officials and so afford to the voters the opportunity of exercising more discrimination in their use of the franchise." The short ballot movement, therefore, called for a reduction in the number of offices and issues voted upon as well as a reduction in the number of candidates who could run for each office. But in order to create a short ballot, more rigorous requirements had to be imposed to prevent potential candidates from qualifying for access to the ballot. These requirements took the form of laws that increased the number of nominating petitions that had to be filed by potential candidates while reducing the amount of time available for gathering the petitions; that required nominating petitions to be gathered from a variety of geographic areas within a state; and that imposed expensive filing fees on potential candidates. All of these requirements functioned as concomitant limitations on access to the ballot. In recent years, however, laws which were designed to effectuate the short "Australian" ballot have come into sharp conflict with contemporary claims that the ballot should be more accessible to minor parties and independent candidates. It is that conflict which is the subject of this chapter.

Does the constitution protect the right of a third party or an independent candidate to a place on the ballot?

Prior to 1968, the courts recognized little or no constitutional protection for minority party or independent candidates seeking a place on the ballot. In *Williams* v. *Rhodes*,[2] however, the Supreme Court was confronted with a series of Ohio laws which rendered it virtually impossible for any candidate other than a Republican or Democrat to obtain ballot status. In *Williams,* supporters of George Wallace had collected over 400,000 signatures on his nominating petition, but were nevertheless unable to place his name on the ballot. Faced with such an obvious perversion of the democratic process, the Supreme Court invalidated the Ohio provisions and enunciated, for the first time, the basic constitutional right of a minority party or an independent to a fair opportunity to appear on the ballot. Even as it was enunciating the basic right, however, the Court recognized that access to the ballot could be restricted to candidates who were able to demonstrate a minimum level of public support. Thus, after *Williams,* the principal questions in the area have turned on the propriety of the various nomination requirements used to measure the required minimum level of support.

How many signatures may election officials require a candidate to collect in order to obtain a place on the ballot?

Most states require prospective candidates to demonstrate a minimum level of support by collecting signatures on a nominating petition. So long as the amount of signatures required does not render it improbable that a "reasonably diligent" candidate will be able to satisfy it, the minimum figure will be sustained. The figure is often expressed in terms of a percentage of the vote cast for the office in the preceding election. In *Williams* v. *Rhodes,* the Court invalidated a 15 percent requirements as too high, but in *Jenness* v. *Fortson,*[3] the court sustained a 5 percent requirement as constitutional. Lower courts have tended to sustain requirements of 5 percent or less, while requirements in excess of 5 percent have been invalidated.[4] In *Storer* v. *Brown,*[5] however, the Court remanded California's 5 percent requirement for further examination of its practical impact on minority parties. The Court stressed that the time period within which the 5 percent figure must be satisfied and the size of the eligible pool of signatories were relevant in determining whether the minimum figure unduly burdened access to the ballot.

How long a period must election officials allow a candidate to circulate his or her nominating petitions?

Obviously, the time period required to obtain nominating signatures varies directly with the number of signatures required. In *Jenness* v. *Fortson,* a 6-month period to satisfy a 5 percent requirement was deemed ample. In *American Party of Texas* v. *White,*[6] a 55-day period to satisfy a 1 percent requirement was upheld by the Supreme Court. In *Williams* v. *Rhodes,* a 15 percent requirement which had to be satisfied by the February preceding the November election was deemed invalid, and one district court has invalidated a petition procedure granting 21 days to obtain 35,000 signatures (2 percent).[7] In *Storer* v. *Brown,* the Supreme Court remanded California's rules, which give minority parties 24 days to meet a 5 percent requirement of approximately 300,000 signatures for additional consideration.

Who may sign a candidate's nominating petition?

Typically, any currently registered voter may sign a nominating petition for a third-party or independent candidate, regardless of the voter's own party affiliation. Confining signatories of nominating petitions to registered voters is probably constitutional, since it would be extremely difficult to check the authenticity and qualifications of unregistered voters. However, attempts to limit the pool of potential signatories to persons registered to vote at the last preceding general election, have been declared unconstitutional.[8] Thus, the traditional practice of approaching unregistered voters, inducing them to register and securing their signatures on third-party nominating petitions remains valid. In *Storer* v. *Brown* and *American Party of Texas* v. *White,* the Supreme Court ruled that persons who have already voted in a major-party primary election may be forbidden to sign a third-party or independent nominating petition. The Court reasoned that it would be unfair to permit a voter to exercise two bites at the nomination process by voting, first, in a party primary, and then signing an independent nominating petition. Similarly, election officials may restrict voters to signing one petition for each office.

In *Storer,* the Court ruled that the ultimate validity

of the nominating petition process would turn on the number of signatures required; the length of time available to secure the signatures; and the size and nature of the pool of eligible signatories. If a combination of those factors unfairly hinders a minority party or independent candidate, the process should not withstand constitutional scrutiny.

Where nominating petitions are required, is it permissible to demand that the residences of those signing be distributed throughout the state?

Some states provide that where nominating petitions are required of candidates for statewide office, the residences of the signers must be geographically distributed throughout the state according to a specified formula. Thus, for example, until 1970 the New York Election Law required that an independent candidate for statewide office must file nominating petitions containing 12,000 signatures signed by at least 50 persons from each of the 62 counties in the state. Such provisions are commonly called "geographical distribution" requirements, and their constitutionality depends upon how such requirements are worded.

In 1969 the Supreme Court invalidated an Illinois law that compelled independent candidates to file signatures of 200 qualified voters from at least 50 of the 102 counties within the state.[9] In defense of its law, Illinois argued that the source of a candidate's support should not be exclusively concentrated in one or two areas, but rather that persons seeking to appear on the ballot should be required to demonstrate that they have a modicum of support throughout the state. The Supreme Court found this defense inadequate in the face of the claim that the Illinois law conferred greater voting strength upon the less populous counties at the expense of the more populated. The Court therefore utilized a "one person-one vote" rationale and invalidated the Illinois law upon the conclusion that it "discriminates against the residents of the populous counties of the State in favor of rural sections."

But even after the Supreme Court's invalidation of the Illinois law, several questions remain regarding the constitutionality of "geographic distribution" provisions. In the Illinois case the Supreme Court unquestionably held that a county-by-county distribution requirement as applied to independent candidates was unconstitutional. But what if such a requirement were imposed not upon independent candidates but upon political parties seeking access to the ballot? It can be argued that while an independent candidate should not be required to demonstrate wide geographic support, an organization calling itself a political party should qualify as a political party only by demonstrating that it has a statewide organization or, at least, statewide acceptance. In partial reliance upon such a distinction, one Federal district court upheld a Utah law that had imposed a "geographical distribution" requirement upon political parties but not upon independent candidates.[10]

A second unresolved question is whether a law that requires that signatures be distributed among election districts rather than counties is constitutional. In the aftermath of the Supreme Court decision in the Illinois case and in reliance upon that case, a New York Federal court invalidated a New York law that had required independent nominating petitions to be signed by at least 50 voters from each county.[11] Upon the judicial interdiction of New York's geographical distribution law, the New York legislature amended the provision and instead of requiring that some signatories reside in each county, the new law imposes a geographical distribution requirement on the basis of congressional districts. Since such a provision does not violate "one person-one vote" principles, it may well be constitutional. However, attempts to impose maximums on signatures from a given county have been invalidated.[12]

Can states legitimately condition access to the ballot upon payment of a filing fee?

Unless there are alternative accessible procedures by which a person unable to afford the filing fee can gain access to the ballot, the filing fee law would be regarded as unconstitutional.

In 1970 a Texas law imposed a filing fee upon all candidates who wanted their names to appear on the ballot in primary elections. Pursuant to this law, filing fees in Texas usually were more than $1,000, often exceeded $5,000, and occasionally were as high as $8,000. Several potential candidates who could not afford these fees challenged the Texas provision. In *Bullock* v. *Carter*,[13] a unanimous Supreme Court invalidated the Texas filing fee requirement with the observation that "the very size of the fees imposed under the Texas system gives it a patently exclusionary character. Many potential office seekers lacking both personal wealth and affluent backers are in every practical sense precluded from seeking the nomination of their chosen party, no matter how qualified they might be, and no matter how broad or enthusiastic their popular support." Thus, the Court in *Bullock* emphasized that the Texas law disadvantaged poor persons, and the Court consequently concluded that "a system that utilizes ability to pay as a condition to being on the ballot, thus [excludes] some candidates otherwise qualified and [denies] an undetermined number of voters the opportunity to vote for candidates of their choice."

The Texas filing fees were obviously excessive. But even more modest fees can have an exclusionary effect. A California provision imposed filing fees for primary as well as general elections upon candidates for congressional, state, and county offices. The California law also provided that write-in votes would not be counted unless the person desiring to be a write-in candidate were to file a statement to that effect and pay the requisite filing fee. Persons who wanted to run in the 1972 primary election but who were unable to pay the required filing fee brought suit and in *Lubin* v. *Panish* [14] the Supreme Court invalidated California's filing fee law. Rather than rest its decision on a finding of discrimination against poorer candidates, as the Court in *Bullock* had done, the judicial opinion in the *Lubin* case emphasized that the California law abridged the right to run for office. Nevertheless, the Court in *Lubin* reached the same conclusion as the *Bullock* court and held that in "the absence of a reasonable means of ballot access, a State may not consistent with constitutional standards, require from an indigent candidate filing fees he cannot pay."

Although both the *Lubin* and *Bullock* cases were brought by persons who were denied the right to run in primary elections, it would seem that the reasoning of the Court in these two cases would be equally applicable to general elections. Somewhat less clear, in the aftermath of the *Lubin* decision, was whether a person who could afford the filing fee but who did not want to pay it had to be allowed some alternative method for qualifying for the ballot. Such an issue arose in Delaware where candidates who were financially capable of paying the fee refused to do so and challenged the filing fee requirement. The Delaware Supreme Court limited the ruling of the *Lubin* and *Bullock* cases to persons who could not afford the filing fee and accordingly upheld the Delaware law. The case was appealed to the United States Supreme Court, which affirmed the decision of the Delaware court without writing an opinion. [15]

NOTES

1. The description of the formalities of the *viva voce* method, as quoted in the text, is found in J.S. Wise, *The End of an Era* 55–56 (1899). General discussions regarding the introduction of the Australian secret ballot in the United States are contained in Key, *Politics, Parties & Pressure Groups* 638–647 (5th ed., 1964) and Harris, *Election Administration in the United States* (1934). A more detailed chronology of the Australian ballot is presented in E.C. Evans, *A History of the Australian Ballot System in the United States* (1917). John Stuart Mill argues in favor of the retention of non-secret voting in Chapter X of his work entitled *Representative Government* (1862). Herbert Croly's claims regarding the advantages of the short ballot are quoted in the text above from H.D. Croly *Progressive Democracy* 289 (1914).

2. 393 U.S. 23 (1968).

3. 403 U.S. 431 (1971).

4. E.g. Lendall v. Bryant, 387 F. Supp. 397 (E.D. Ark. 1975) (15 percent—invalid); SLP v. Rhodes, 318 F. Supp. 1262 (S.D. Ohio 1970), app dism. as moot sub nom Gilligan v. Sweetenham, 405 U.S. 949 (1972) (7 percent—invalid); Williams v. Tucker, 382 F. Supp. 381 (M.D. Pa. 1974) (2 percent—valid).

5. 415 U.S. 724 (1974).

6. 415 U.S. 767 (1974).

7. People's Party v. Tucker, 347 F. Supp. 1 (M.D. Pa. 1972)

8. SWP v. Rockefeller, 314 F. Supp. 984 (S.D.N.Y.) aff'd 400 U.S. 806 (1970).

9. Moore v. Ogilvie, 394 U.S. 814 (1969).

10. Zautra v. Miller, 348 F. Supp. 847 (D. Utah 1972).

11. SWP v. Rockefeller, *supra,* note 8.

12. Baird v. Davoren, 346 F. Supp. 515 (D. Mass. 1972) (33 percent maximum on signatures from given county—invalid); SWP v. Hare, 304 F. Supp. 534 (E.D. Mich. 1969) (35 percent maximum—invalid).

13. 405 U.S. 134 (1972).

14. 415 U.S. 709 (1974).
15. Cassidy v. Willis, 323 A2d 598 (Del. 1974) aff'd 419 U.S. 1042 (1974). See also Adams v. Askew, 511 F. 2d 700 (1975).

V

The Right to Fair Representation

Unlike ancient Athens or a present-day New England town, the scope and complexity of American life renders it impossible to permit all citizens to vote directly on all issues. Instead, citizens select representatives who act as proxies in casting votes on the issues which confront society. Ideally, the proper functioning of a free election process guarantees that elected representatives will accurately reflect the wishes of their constituents. However, even the fairest election procedures will not guarantee the proper functioning of a representative democracy unless the system is structured to ensure that the elected "proxies" constitute an accurate microcosm of the underlying political unit. To the extent that certain interests, whether ideological, political, economic, or racial, are over or underrepresented, the ideals of representative democracy are seriously compromised. In recent years, the Supreme Court has struggled, with varying degrees of success, to articulate and administer basic principles of fair

representation which must exist to permit our form of
democracy to function properly.

Does the Constitution guarantee fair representation?

Not explicitly. For many years courts declined to
consider whether legislative representation was fair.
Finally, in 1962, in *Baker* v. *Carr* [1] the Supreme Court
ruled that legislative representation must be fairly apportioned on a population basis.

In *Baker* v. *Carr*, a Tennessee voter complained that
the state legislature had not been reapportioned in
many years, resulting in gross disparities in population
between legislative districts. The Supreme court, re-
versing its prior decisions, ruled that voters were constitutionally entitled to legislative districts of equal
population.

The Supreme Court has never ruled that legislative
representation, if apportioned fairly as to population,
must accurately reflect racial, political, economic, or
ideological groupings in a given district. Of course,
overt attempts to manipulate the electoral process to
deprive minority groups of fair representation have
been declared unlawful by the Supreme Court.

Given the reluctance of the Supreme Court to articulate a requirement that representatives must accurately
mirror the population they purport to represent, and
given the difficulty of proving an overt discriminatory
motive in many cases of suspected electoral manipulation, the bulk of the law of fair representation has
developed pursuant to the Supreme Court's command
in *Baker* v. *Carr* that, at least, legislative representation should be apportioned on a "one person-one vote"
basis.

What does "One Person-One Vote" Mean?

The principle of one person-one vote requires that
whenever a representative deliberative body is estab-

lished, each member of the deliberative body should represent an equal number of persons.

What evil was the "One Person-One Vote" rule designed to eradicate?

Imagine a state legislature made up of three persons. Legislator A is elected from a district containing 20 percent of the state's population; legislator B from a district containing 25 percent, and legislator C from a district containing 55 percent of the state's population. The laws of such a state can be made by legislators A and B over the opposition of legislator C, despite the fact that legislators A and B are "proxies" for only 45 percent of the state's population, while legislator C is "proxy" for 55 percent. Prior to the Supreme Court's "one person-one vote" decision in 1962, many legislative bodies reflected just such an imbalance, caused primarily by a failure to redraw district lines to reflect substantial rural to urban population shifts. The "one person-one vote" rule sought to assure that deliberative bodies would consist of legislators representing an equal number of citizens, guaranteeing that laws could be made only with the acquiescence of "proxies" representing at least 50 percent of the state's population.

Why did the Supreme Court use the phrase "One Person-One Vote" instead of "Equal or Proportionate Representation"?

The Supreme Court was confronted with the fact that the Constitution does not explicitly assure numerically fair representation. Rather than imply such a right, the Court elected to rely upon the constitutional requirement that no state may deny equal protection of the laws. If we assume that in our imaginary state consisting of 100 persons, legislator A is elected by 20 voters; B by 25 voters; and C by 55 voters, then each voter in legislator A's district has a 1/20 say in who is elected; yet each voter in legislator C's district would have only a 1/55 say in the election of his or her legislator. The Supreme Court was able to condemn such obvious inequality in relative voting power between the individual voters of the two districts as a denial of equal protection of the laws. Ironically, however, the evil at issue was not so much inequality of relative voting power between the individual residents of the various districts, as the distortion of the representative democratic process caused by the lack of numerically proportionate representation.

Doesn't the United States Senate violate the "One Person-One Vote" principle?

Since every state is entitled to two senators regardless of population, the makeup of the senate is in clear violation of the one person-one vote principle. However, the Supreme Court has recognized that one of the unique historical factors which induced the original 13 sovereign colonies to federate into the United States was a political compromise which assured the less populous states of two senators.[2] Thus, the Senate is the only general legislative body which has been exempted from the operation of the "one person-one vote" principle.

Must both houses of a Bicameral State Legislature be apportioned in accordance with "One Person-One Vote"?

Yes.[3] Many persons have argued that one house of a bicameral state legislature should enjoy an exemption from the one person-one vote principle, similar to the exemption recognized for the United States Senate. However, the Supreme Court has rejected such an exemption on that ground that the senatorial exemption stems from the unique factors inherent in the union of sovereign colonies into a Federal union. Since the subdivisions represented in state legislatures never enjoyed independent sovereign existence, no similar exemption would be justified. Thus, both houses of a state legislature must comply with one person-one vote.

What government bodies does the "One Person-One Vote" principle apply to?

Broadly speaking, the "one person-one vote" principle applies to all elected representative bodies exercising general government functions. Specifically, "one person-one vote" has been held applicable to the United States House of Representatives; [4] both houses of a state legislature; [5] county, town, village, and municipal legislatures; [6] local school boards; [7] local boards of election; and certain indian tribal elections.

Are any elected representative bodies exempt from "One Person-One Vote"?

In addition to the exemption for the United States Senate, the Supreme Court has recognized that certain local bodies exercising extremely limited powers (such as water improvement districts and off-track betting authorities) may apportion representation on a basis other than population. [8] Elected school boards, however, continue to be subject to "one person-one vote." [9]

Does "One Person-One Vote" apply to the election of judges?

Although the Supreme Court has never issued a plenary opinion on the point, most authorities have exempted judicial elections from the one person-one vote principle on the understandable ground that judges do not perform as proxies in the representative democratic process. [10] However, to the extent that judicial resources are misallocated on an unfair basis, an independent violation of the Constitution may exist.

Does the "One Person-One Vote" principle apply to appointive, rather than elective, bodies?

The one person-one vote rule has been held inapplicable to an appointed school board.[11] However, to the extent that the body performs traditional legislative functions, even an appointive membership would probably be tested against the one person-one vote principle.[12]

Does the "One Person-One Vote" principle apply to nominating petitions?

Yes. The Supreme Court has invalidated a scheme which required a fixed number of petition signatures from counties of varying population on the ground that voters in the least populous counties were given a disproportionate say in the nominating process.[13]

Does the "One Person-One Vote" principle apply to the selection of delegates to political party nominating conventions?

Although the Supreme Court has expressed doubt,[14] and although the lower courts have not been unanimous,[15] the bulk of existing authority favors the application of the one person-one vote principle to national party nominating conventions and to local units of political parties engaged in the nominating process.[16]

However, the courts have recognized that some flexibility must be permitted to political parties in apportioning convention delegates. Thus, lower Federal courts have upheld "bonus" provisions which provide additional delegates for states which supported the party's candidate in the preceding general election. Moreover, courts have permitted the apportionment to be based upon party registration rather than raw population.

What population base must be used to determine

whether the "One Person-One Vote" principle has been satisfied?

Ordinarily, representation is apportioned on the basis of the most recent United States census figures. However, whenever a state carries out a more accurate population survey, its figures may be substituted. Attempts to apportion on the basis of registered or eligible voters, rather than on the basis of residents, have been consistently rejected, in the absence of special circumstances.[17] College students are deemed residents of their college communities for apportionment purposes.

Must absolute mathematical equality exist in order to satisfy the "One Person-One Vote" principle?

Absolute mathematical equality is impossible. The degree of permissible deviation varies with the nature of the government unit and the justification offered to explain the deviation from strict mathematical equality.

What is the permissible deviation from mathematical equality in apportioning membership in the House of Representatives?

The Supreme Court has consistently required adherence to strict mathematical equality in apportioning representation in the House of Representatives.[18] The Court bases its insistence upon strict mathematical equality upon the command of Article I, Section 2 of the Constitution that "[t]he House of Representatives shall be composed of Members chosen every year by the people of the several states. . . ." Application of strict equality has resulted in the invalidation of congressional apportionment plans guilty of population deviations as small as a maximum of 4 percent with an average deviation of 3,421 persons per 460,000 residents. Under current population figures, each member of the House represents approximately 460,000 residents.

What is the maximum permissible deviation from mathematical equality in apportioning state legislatures and other statewide bodies subject to "One Person-One Vote"?

Prior to 1973, many courts had held state legislative apportionment to the same strict standards which govern congressional reapportionment. However, in 1973, the Supreme Court upheld a Virginia state legislative reapportionment which exhibited a maximum population deviation of 16.4 percent on the ground that it achieved "substantial equality" while preserving legitimate state concern with maintaining the integrity of local political subdivisions.[19] In 1975 the Supreme Court declined to approve a North Dakota legislative apportionment which exhibited a maximum deviation of 20 percent despite the state concern with avoiding districts bisected by the Missouri River.[20] Thus, to the extent significant and legitimate state concerns require some deviation from strict mathematical equality, so long as "substantial equality" is achieved, deviations of up to a maximum of 16.4 percent may be tolerated. However, deviations in excess of 16.4 percent, even if justified by a legitimate state concern, will probably not be permitted.

Must all deviations from mathematical equality be justified by a countervailing state interest?

No. Prior to 1973, most courts assumed that all deviations from strict mathematical equality imposed a heavy burden of justification on the state. However, in 1973, the Supreme Court upheld a Connecticut reapportionment plan exhibiting an 8 percent maximum deviation and a Texas plan exhibiting a 9.9 percent deviation without requiring any state justification.[21] Accordingly, it now appears that the Supreme Court views population deviations in state apportionment plans of up to 10 percent as sufficiently small to require no justification; of between 10 and 16.4 percent as large enough to require substantial state justification; and of over 17 percent to be impermissible, even if supported by substantial state justification. Despite its more permissive attitude toward state legislative reapportionment, the Supreme Court has continued to insist on strict mathematical equality in congressional apportionment.

What is the maximum permissible deviation from mathematical equality in apportioning local legislative bodies?

Even before the relaxation of state standards in 1973, the Supreme Court had upheld a county apportionment plan exhibiting a maximum population deviation of 12 percent caused by the county's attempt to respect the boundary lines of its constituent towns.[22] Although no local case has reached the Supreme Court since the 1973 term, given the relaxation of the principle of strict mathematical equality in statewide reapportionment, a similar relaxation may be anticipated on the local level.

If a legislature fails to apportion itself properly, may a court redraw district lines?

Yes. It is now clear that courts are empowered to impose a redistricting plan upon legislatures which are unable or unwilling to apportion themselves properly. However, before imposing a court plan, a judge should permit the legislature a reasonable opportunity to draw its own lines. Moreover, if a court finds it necessary to impose its own plan, it must conform as closely as possible to any unsuccessful legislative plan. Finally, courts may not impose multi-member districts as part of a judicially imposed reapportionment.

Does the strict application of the "One Person-One Vote" principle assure fair representation?

Not necessarily. Many devices which meet even the strictest standard of mathematical equality can effectively deprive minority groups of fair representation. Thus, while the enunciation and enforcement of a one person-one vote principle was an important step in assuring the proper functioning of a representative democracy, it was far from a panacea. Among the devices which threaten the ideal of fair representation, while fully satisfying the one person-one vote principle, are gerrymanders (both racial and political); multi-member districts and at-large constituencies; and super-majority requirements.

What is a gerrymander and how does it endanger the principle of fair representation?

Gerrymanders are named for a Massachusetts politician, Ellsbridge Gerry, who created a legislative district shaped like a salamander in order to include pockets of his supporters and exclude his opponents. The drawing of district lines in a conscious attempt to include or exclude given voters has since been known as gerrymandering. If we return to our imaginary state of 100 voters, strict compliance with the one person-one vote principle would call for legislative districts of 33, 33 and 34 persons. If we assume a minority group (either racial or political) population of 36, living in a contiguous geographical area, proper operation of the principle of fair representation would result in a legislature with one of the three seats controlled by the minority group. However, if the district lines are "gerrymandered" to place a segment of the minority bloc equally in each of the three districts, the minority will be outvoted in each district by 21 or 22 to 12 and will lose all representation in the legislature.

Moreover, if we assume a "minority" population of

55, proper operation of the principle of fair representation would result in a legislature narrowly controlled by the "minority" group. However, if district lines are drawn to divide the "minority" population into three districts in a 30–12–13 distribution, the minority group will control one seat in the resulting legislature, while being outvoted in the remaining two districts. The potential for manipulation inherent in the gerrymander has not been lost on American politicians and much of the malfunctioning in our democratic process results from the cynical drawing of district lines, not to assure fair representation, but to perpetuate the political status quo.

May districts be gerrymandered to deprive racial minorities of fair representation?

No. The Supreme Court has repeatedly ruled that the intentional drawing of district lines to minimize the political power of racial minorities is a violation of the Constitution.[23] However, it is extremely difficult to prove that gerrymandering which has a detrimental effect on racial minorities was intended to have such an effect. Accordingly, while many courts have struggled to protect racial minorities from gerrymandering, a disturbing tendency to accept disguised racial gerrymanders continues to exist.

May districts be gerrymandered to augment or insure control by a racial minority?

Courts have divided over the legality of "benign gerrymanders" designed to augment or consolidate the political position of racial minorities.[24] No clear answer is possible: however, the result may differ depending upon the degree of past discrimination, the applicability of the Voting Rights Act (discussed *infra,* in Chapter VI) and the fairness of the resulting legislative mix.

May "political" factors be included in the drawing of district lines?

Prior to 1973, many persons argued that the inclusion of political factors in the drawing of district lines was precisely the evil which permitted gerrymandering to flourish. However, in 1973, the Supreme Court upheld the inclusion of political factors in the apportionment process.[25] The result has been a spate of "political" apportionments exhibiting an overwhelming number of "safe" seats for each major party, with a resultant freezing of the political status quo. Indeed, many political scientists argue that the avowedly political reapportionments sanctioned by the Supreme Court result in legislatures even less receptive to fluctuations in the popular will than were the glaringly malapportioned legislatures which preceded them. Of course, if a dominant political group were to utilize the gerrymander in a blatant manner to freeze out its opposition (instead of cooperating with the opposition to provide "safe" seats for each), some degree of judicial relief would probably be available.

Is there any check on the practice of political gerrymandering?

Traditional requirements that legislative districts be "contiguous" and "compact" provide some protection from the most blatant gerrymanders, as does the one person-one vote principle. However, under the current Supreme Court guidelines, control over political gerrymandering remains minimal.

What is a multi-member district and how does it endanger the principle of fair representation?

In a multi-member district, a number of representatives are elected at large by an enlarged geographical entity which would ordinarily be divided into single member districts. In our imaginary state with 100 voters, if 30 percent of the electorate is minority and 70 percent majority, the proper operation of the representative process should enable minority voters to control one seat in the three-person legislature. However, if the state were to adopt a multi-member constituency, all three members of the legislature would be elected by all the voters of the state, depriving the 30 percent bloc of any representation in the legislature.

Are multi-member districts unlawful when they dilute the political power of racial minorities?

To the extent a multi-member district deprives a submerged racial minority of meaningful access to the political process, the Supreme Court has branded them unconstitutional.[26] However, the Court has ruled that multi-member districts are not facially unconstitutional and the mere fact that a racial minority would fare better politically under a single-member scheme will not automatically invalidate a multi-member district.[27] In determining whether a multi-member district impermissibly discriminates against minorities, the Supreme Court weighs the following factors: (a) the history of past discrimination against the submerged minority, especially in connection with participation in the political process; (b) the extent of minority participation in the candidate selection process; (c) the absence of ameliorative techniques such as "bullet voting," designed to permit minority representation; (d) the failure of members of the submerged minority to win elective office in the recent past; and (e) the failure of elected representatives to provide adequate representation of the submerged minority. Despite the Court's attempt at guidance, the line between a permissible multi-member district and one which invidiously discriminates against submerged minorities will doubtless prove difficult to draw.

Are multi-member districts unlawful when they dilute the political power of political minorities?

Probably not. The Supreme Court has consistently ruled that multi-member districts are not facially unconstitutional. The lack of success in challenging gerrymandering on political, as opposed to racial, grounds, does not bode well for similar challenges to multi-member districting.

What ameliorative devices exist for protecting minority voters in a multi-member constituency?

A number of ameliorative devices can be built in to a multi-member system to avoid submerging a minority voting bloc. First, "bullet voting," which enables minority voters to cast votes for a single favored candidate despite multiple vacancies, thereby increasing that candidate's chances of election; second, "limited voting," which places maximums on the number of candidates which a given voter can support, ensuring that the majority bloc of voters cannot control all the vacancies; third, "limited candidacy," which places maximums on the candidates which a given political party can offer; and fourth, residence requirements, which require candidates elected on an at-large basis to reside in various subdivisions throughout the district.

What is weighted voting?

Closely related to multi-member districts is the concept of weighted voting which permits representatives to cast votes in direct proportion to the population of their districts. The complexity of weighted voting schemes can be so difficult to plot that many courts require computer assistance in passing upon their legality. Moreover, weighted voting threatens to submerge minority voting blocs by depriving them of a meaningful voice in the election of a representative, even though, once elected, the representative casts a properly weighted vote. Thus, in our imaginary state, if District A contains 20 voters, District B contains 35 voters, and District C contains 55 voters, a weighted voting scheme would permit the respective representatives to cast a vote directly proportionate to the population he or she represents. While such a scheme would preclude distortion of the representative pattern, it would not cure the fact that each voter in District A has a 1/20 voice in electing a representative, while voters in District C have only a 1/55 voice.

Are supermajority requirements lawful?

Yes. The Supreme Court has ruled that so long as it is not a discriminatory device aimed at a discrete minority, supermajority requirements are not unlawful.[28] Of course, if a supermajority requirement appears aimed at a discrete racial minority or if it unfairly acts to prevent the protection of racial minorities, it will be invalidated.[29]

NOTES

1. Baker v. Carr, 369 U.S. 186 (1962).
2. Reynolds v. Sims, 377 U.S. 533 (1964).
3. Reynolds v. Sims, *supra.*
4. Wesberry v. Sanders, 376 U.S. 1 (1964).
5. Reynolds v. Sims, *supra.*
6. Gray v. Sanders, 372 U.S. 368 (1963); Avery v. Midland County, 390 U.S. 474 (1968).
7. Hadley v. Junior College District, 397 U.S. 50 (1970).
8. Salyer Land Co. v. Tulare Lake Basin Water Storage Co., 410 U.S. 719 (1973).
9. E.g. Panoir v. Iberville Parish School Board, 498 F. 2d 1232 (5th Cir. 1974); Rosenthal v. Board of Education, 497 F2d 726 (2d. Cir. 1974).
10. E.g. Wells v. Edwards, 409 U.S. 1095 (1973) aff'g 347 F. Supp. 453 (M.D. La. 1972).

11. Sailors v. Kent Board of Education, 387 U.S. 105 (1967).
12. Ortiz v. Colon, 385 F. Supp. 111 (D.P.R. 1974).
13. Moore v. Ogilvie, 394 U.S. 814 (1969).
14. O'Brien v. Brown, 409 U.S. 1 (1972). See also Cousins v. Wigoda, 419 U.S. 477 (1975).
15. Compare Todd v. Oklahoma State Democratic Committee, 361 F. Supp. 491 (W.D. Okla. 1973) with Redfearn v. Delaware Republican State Committee, 502 F. 2nd 1123 (3d Cir. 1974).
16. E.g. Seergy v. Kings County Republican County Committee, 459 F2d 308 (2d Cir. 1972).
17. Burns v. Richardson, 384 U.S. 73 (1966); Mahan v. Howell, 410 U.S. 315 (1973).
18. White v. Weiser, 410 U.S. 783 (1973).
19. Mahan v. Howell, 410 U.S. 315 (1973).
20. Chapman v. Meier, 420 U.S. 1 (1975).
21. Gaffney v. Cummings, 412 U.S. 735 (1973); White v. Regester, 412 U.S. 755 (1973).
22. Abate v. Mundt, 403 U.S. 182 (1971).
23. Gomillion v. Lightfoot, 364 U.S. 339 (1960).
24. E.g. United Jewish Organizations v. Wilson, 510 F. 2d 512 (2d. Cir. 1975) cert. granted   U.S. (1975) (upholding benign gerrymander).
25. Gaffney v. Cummings, 412 U.S. 755 (1973).
26. White v. Regester, 412 U.S. 755 (1973).
27. Whitcomb v. Chavis, 403 U.S. 124 (1971).
28. Gordon v. Lance, 403 U.S. 1 (1971).
29. Reitman v. Mulkey, 387 U.S. 369 (1967); Hunter v. Erickson, 393 U.S. 385 (1969).

VI

Congressional Protection of the Right to Vote

The evolution of judicial protection of the right to vote has been a relatively recent phenomenon. Prior to the enunciation of an expanded vision of the Equal Protection Clause by Chief Justice Warren in *Kramer* v. *Union Free School District No. 15*,[1] the lack of an obvious doctrinal base had severely hampered attempts to utilize the courts as forums for the protection of voting rights—e.g. *Pope* v. *Williams*,[2] (upholding durational residence requirements for voting). As the material in the earlier chapters demonstrates, the application by the Warren court of strict equal protection review to statutes which selectively distribute the franchise wrought a virtual revolution in the judicial response to voting rights.

However, the Warren court's enunciation of new doctrine was not universally accepted. Even within the Court itself, Justices Stewart, Harlan, and Black questioned the appropriateness of utilizing the Equal Protection Clause as a substitute for a nonexistent explicit general constitutional guarantee of voting rights. Reaction by foes of the Warren court was doubly critical, especially since many of its most controversial decisions in other areas were based upon a similarly revitalized notion of the Equal Protection Clause. With the passing of the Warren court majority, only Justices Brennan, Marshall, and perhaps, Powell seem prepared to apply the Warren court voting precedents with full vigor. The remainder of the Court, while unquestionably influenced by the increased general concern for voting rights which was both the cause and an effect of the Warren court decisions, remains seriously divided over the appropriate judicial response to the problem. Chief Justice Burger and Justices Stewart and White appear to have retreated from some implications of the many Warren court voting precedents, while continuing to respect them in a general sense, while Justices Rehnquist and Blackmun occasionally appear prepared to vote as though the revolution in judicial protection of voting rights had never occurred. Thus, the unstable doctrinal basis which underlies much of the current judicial protection of voting rights counsels caution in relying too heavily on the courts as sole vindicators of the right to vote.

Moreover, given the basic requirement that the judiciary confine itself to a case-by-case approach; the cumbersome and expensive aspects of any litigation campaign; and the serious difficulties in formulating effective judicial relief, increasing pressure has been placed on the legislature to formulate effective responses to the unpleasant fact that even after the Warren court revolution only about one-half the eligible voters participate in our political life. Legislative response to the problem has centered on congressional passage and amendment of the Voting Rights Act of 1965 and sporadic state legislative reform of the registration process.

What is the Voting Rights Act of 1965?

The Voting Rights Act of 1965 consists of three blocs of legislation enacted in 1965, 1970, and 1975, respectively, which provide the major congressional protection of the right to vote.[3] The Voting Rights Act is divided into two general segments: one which provides substantive protection of the right to vote by prescribing national norms for certain elements of the electoral process (such as absentee balloting in presidential elections and bilingual ballots for linguistic minorities) and one which zeroes in on geographical areas where participation in the electoral process has dipped below 50 percent of the eligible voting population to ensure that election laws are not manipulated to the detriment of minority voters. The current statute was extended on August 6, 1975 through August 6, 1982. Unfortunately, the internal complexity of the Voting Rights Act renders many of its provisions indecipherable to lawyers and laypersons alike.

How does the Voting Rights Act prevent the manipulation of election laws to the detriment of disenfranchised voters?

Once a given political subdivision has been deemed subject to the special sub-50 percent participation provisions of the Voting Rights Act, no changes in its laws or practices affecting voting may go into effect without the prior permission of the attorney general of the United States or a three-judge district court in the District of Columbia.[4] This requirement of "pre-clearance" of new laws relating to voting is designed to guarantee that election laws will not be modified to continue to freeze out persons who had been disenfranchised in the past. The operation of the "pre-clearance" provisions of the Voting Rights Act raise at least the following questions: When does a political subdivision fall under the pre-clearance provisions of the Voting Rights Act? What types of changes in election law require "pre-clearance"? What standards determine whether the Attorney General or the court should grant pre-clearance? What are the consequences of a failure of a political subdivision to obtain pre-clearance? Who may complain of a failure to obtain pre-clearance? What are the mechanics of obtaining pre-clearance? How may a covered subdivision remove itself from the pre-clearance provisions of the Act? Is a requirement of Federal pre-clearance of state election laws constitutional?

When does a political subdivision fall under the pre-clearance provisions of the Voting Rights Act?

Two separate requirements must exist before a political subdivision is deemed subject to the pre-clearance provisions of the Voting Rights Act.

First, the director of the census must certify that fewer than 50 percent of the eligible voting-age population registered or voted in any one of the 1964, 1968, or 1972 presidential elections. If statewide figures fall below the 50 percent mark, the entire state may fall under the pre-clearance requirements of the Act. If 50 percent participation is not achieved in a smaller political subdivision—such as a county—in which voter registration is administered, the smaller political subdivision may be deemed subject to pre-clearance. Thus, although New York State clearly exceeds the 50 percent figure on a statewide basis, three counties—Bronx, Kings, and New York—have been placed under pre-clearance control because of the disappointing voter participation in those counties. Once a political subdivision smaller than a state is deemed subject to pre-clearance, any law of statewide application which affects voting in the covered subdivisions must receive pre-clearance from the attorney general before going into effect in the covered subdivision. Thus far, counties and towns are the smallest political subdivisions to which the 50 percent test has been applied. If local law administers voter registration on a basis other than county by county, or town by town, no impediment to examining even smaller political subdivisions for 50 percent participation would seem to exist.

Even if the political subdivision in question (state, county, or local) fails the 50 percent participation test, a second precondition must exist in order to invoke the pre-clearance remedy. The subdivision must have a recent history of having utilized a "test or device" as a prerequisite for registration or voting. As originally drafted in 1965, "test or device" meant literacy requirements, educational tests, and amorphous good moral character and vouching in requirements.[5]

Under the original 1965 definition, the following political subdivisions were placed, and currently remain, under pre-clearance supervision: Alabama, Georgia, Louisiana, Mississippi, South Carolina, Virginia, 39 counties in North Carolina—Anson, Beaufort, Bladen, Camden, Caswell, Chowen, Cleveland, Craven, Cumberland, Edgecomb, Franklin, Gatson, Gates, Granville, Greene, Guilford, Halifax, Harnett, Hertford, Hoke, Lee, Lenoir, Martin, Nash, Northampton, Orslow, Pasquotank, Perquamins, Person, Pitt, Robeson, Rockingham, Scotland, Union, Vance, Wake, Washington, Wayne, and Wilson; 9 counties in Arizona—Apache, Cochise, Coconino, Mohave, Navajo, Pima, Pinal, Santa Cruz, and Yuma; 2 counties in California—Monterrey and Yuba; one county in Idaho—Elmore; 3 counties in New York—Bronx, Kings, and New York; and one county in Wyoming—Campbell.

The 1975 extension of the Act established a potentially significant addition to the definition of "test or device." From and after August 6, 1975, a political subdivision will have been deemed guilty of administering a "test or device" if within 10 years of November 1,

1972 it administered an exclusively English-language registration procedure or election despite the existence of a "linguistic minority" of more than 5 percent of the subdivision's voting-age population.[6]

By expanding the concept of "test or device," the 1975 extension may result in a dramatic increase in the coverage of the pre-clearance provisions of the Act. Since many—if not most—political subdivisions exhibiting voter participation of under 50 percent also contain substantial linguistic minorities, and since bilingual elections were virtually unknown in American politics and until very recently, the net result of the 1975 extension may be to *de facto* impose pre-clearance controls on every political subdivision which fails to demonstrate voter participation in excess of 50 percent of the eligible population. Thus far, the following subdivisions have been added to the list of pre-clearance areas as a consequence of the 1975 Amendment: Alaska; the remainder of Arizona; two additional counties in California—Kings and Merced; one county in Colorado—El Paso; three towns in Connecticut—Groton, Mansfield and Southbury; three counties in Florida—Hardee, Hillsborough and Monroe; one county in Hawaii—Honolulu; one county in Idaho—Elmore; eighteen towns in Maine—Beddington, Carroll Plantation, Caswell Plantation, Charleston, Chelsea, Connor Unorganized Territory, Cutler, Limestone, Ludlow, Nashville Plantation, New Gloucester, Reed Plantation, Winter Harbor and Woodland; nine towns in Massachusetts—Amherst, Ayer, Belchertown, Bourne, Harvard, Sandwich, Shirley, Sunderland and Wrentham; ten towns in New Hampshire—Antrim, Benton, Boscawen, Millsfield Township, Newington, Pinkhams Grant, Rindge, Stewartstown, Stratford and Unity; and one additional county in North Carolina—Bertie (in addition to the 39 counties listed above). Given the fact that once any political subdivision in a state becomes subject to pre-clearance, state election laws affecting that subdivision must also receive pre-clearance, the 1975 extension may well have transformed the Voting Rights Act from a regional device aimed at eliminating racial discrimination in voting in the states of the old Confederacy into a broad national remedy capable of grappling with the disturbing phenomenon of unacceptably small voter turnout wherever it occurs.

What types of changes in election law require pre-clearance?

In *Allen* v. *State Board of Elections, Perkins* v. *Matthews,* and *Georgia* v. *United States,*[7] the Supreme Court directed that the pre-clearance requirements of the Voting Rights Act be given a broad construction to carry out its remedial purpose. Accordingly, courts have held that any change in a covered subdivision's laws or practices which might affect voting or running for office must be submitted to the attorney general for pre-clearance review, including: (a) annexations and related boundary modifications affecting the makeup of the electorate; (b) the substitution of at-large or multi-member elections for single-member constituencies, and vice versa; (c) changes in the location and number of polling places; (d) changes in the method of and requirements for registration; (e) changes in requirements for running for office or obtaining ballot status; (f) alterations in the form of the ballot; (g) changes in the terms and powers of office; (h) special elections; (i) alterations of intraparty rules governing eligibility for primary voting or delegate selection; and (j) reapportionment plans. Of course, such a list is not exhaustive, and any alteration which can be shown to affect voting should fall under the pre-clearance umbrella.

The application of pre-clearance to reapportionment

plans is of potentially great significance. The use of
pre-clearance as a device to force the adoption of district lines favoring minorities is illustrated by the litigation surrounding the Fourteenth Congressional District
in Brooklyn, which was redrawn under the supervision
of the attorney general after the original laws had been
challenged for failure to obtain pre-clearance.[8] Benign
racial gerrymandering to satisfy the strictures of the
pre-clearance provisions of the Voting Rights Act has
been sustained as constitutional, although the issue is
not free from doubt.[9] If the 1975 extension of the Act
leads to the expected geographical expansion in the
scope of pre-clearance, substantial segments of the reapportionment process may be brought under the scrutiny of pre-clearance.

The Supreme Court has ruled that court-directed
changes in a covered subdivision's laws or practices
affecting voting are not subject to pre-clearance.[10]
Thus, a court-imposed reapportionment plan would not
be subject to pre-clearance. Of course, court-imposed
reapportionment plants are subject to judicial review
under peculiarly exacting standards discussed *infra* in
Chapter V.

What are the mechanics of obtaining pre-clearance?

A political subdivision wishing to obtain pre-
clearance of a proposed change in its election laws may
pursue two alternatives. The subdivision may seek administrative pre-clearance by submitting the proposed
alteration to the attorney general. (Such applications
are processed by the Civil Rights Division of the Department of Justice.)[11] The subdivision's application
must set forth the proposed alteration, together with a
demonstration that it does not have the intent nor will
it have the effect of diluting minority electoral participation. Interested persons or groups may comment on

the proposed alteration, urging either grant or rejection of pre-clearance.

The attorney general must act on a request for pre-clearance within 60 days of the proposed alteration's submission. However, the 60 days does not begin to run until the attorney general has received all the information he deems necessary to a decision. Failure to deny pre-clearance within the 60 days permits the alteration to go into effect, subject to right of the attorney general to challenge the alteration on substantive grounds at a later date. Alternatively, if the attorney general declines pre-clearance or if the subdivision elects to bypass the attorney general entirely, a covered subdivision may file an action before a three-judge district court in the United States District Court for the District of Columbia seeking a declaration that the proposed alteration was not intended to and will not have the effect of diluting the electoral participation of minority voters. Affected persons or groups are permitted to intervene in such a declaratory judgement. In the absence of the attorney general's consent, it has proven extremely difficult to secure such a declaration, although the Supreme Court's recent action in overruling the refusal to grant such a declaration, in connection with the annexation of a white enclave by Richmond, Virginia, may presage a relaxation in the area. The Richmond annexation is discussed *infra*.[12]

In 1971, six years after Congress enacted pre-clearance, the attorney general promulgated the first set of regulations governing the submission by affected subdivisions of proposed changes in their laws or practices related to voting, which are set forth in 28 Code of Federal Regulations, pt. 51 (1973). The regulations require covered subdivisions to routinely notify the attorney general of any proposed alterations in election laws. Interested private persons or groups may obtain copies of such routine notifications from the Justice

Department, and thus play an important role in monitoring and enforcing pre-clearance by commenting upon relevant proposed alterations.

If, despite opposition, the attorney general grants pre-clearance of a proposed alteration, courts are divided whether disappointed objectors may seek judicial review of the attorney general's decision. If the decision in question was based upon an erroneous understanding of the Act and of the responsibilities of the attorney general under it, judicial review should be available. Thus, if the attorney general declines to conduct an investigation of the effect of a proposed alteration, or if he applies an erroneous burden of proof or burden of persuasion, a court should be able to apply corrective measures.[13] If, however, the attorney general, applying correct procedures and standards, merely disagrees with objectors over the conclusion to be drawn from the record, judicial review seems more questionable.[14] Of course, even if pre-clearance is granted, the alteration in question may be challenged as violative of the constitutional norms described in earlier chapters.

What standards determine whether either the Attorney General or a court should grant pre-clearance?

The statutory standard imposed by the Voting Rights Act requires that pre-clearance be denied if the proposed alteration was enacted with the purpose of or will have the effect of denying or abridging the right to vote on account of race, color, or membership in a language minority.[15] The enunciation of such a standard raises a number of difficult problems.

First, who has the burden of persuading the attorney general or the United States District Court for the District of Columbia that a proposed alteration does or does not "deny or abridge the right to vote on account of race or color"? In ordinary challenges to the constitutionality of election laws, the complainant is invariably saddled with the burden of persuading a judge by a preponderance of the evidence that a particular statute unconstitutionally discriminates against a given group. When pre-clearance is sought, however, the traditional—and often difficult—burden of proof is shifted from complainants and is imposed instead upon the political subdivision seeking to alter its election law.[16] Thus, in order to persuade the attorney general or a district court to grant pre-clearance, a covered subdivision must persuade the attorney general or the court that the new law was neither intended to deny or abridge, nor will have the effect of denying or abridging, the right to vote on account of race, color, or membership in a language minority.

If the attorney general or the court is in doubt about whether a proposed alteration will deny or abridge the right to vote, he must deny pre-clearance. The propriety of imposing the burden of proof and persuasion upon a covered subdivision was upheld by the Supreme Court in *Georgia* v. *United States* [17] and has been of particular significance in attempts to obtain pre-clearance of proposed legislative reapportionments by covered subdivisions.

Second, what does the phrase "deny or abridge the right to vote" mean? If one were to impose a literal reading of the phrase, proposed alterations which did not overtly discriminate on the basis of race, color, or membership in a language minority might well be deemed satisfactory. However, the courts have, with virtual unanimity, rejected the literal interpretation. Conversely, if one applies a broad reading of the phrase, any alteration in election law which would result in a lessening of a minority group's political power might be deemed ineligible for pre-clearance. Prior to the 1975 term of the Supreme Court, the attorney general and most courts applied the broad reading of the phrase to deny pre-clearance to any alteration when the actual political power of a racial minority would be decreased *de facto* by the alteration. In 1975, however, the solicitor general of the United States, Robert Bork, disavowed the broad reading of "denied or abridged" which had been utilized by a district court in refusing to grant Richmond, Virginia's application for pre-clearance to annex a white enclave. The district court had reasoned that since, prior to annexation, black voters would have constituted 55 percent of Richmond's electorate, while after the annexation blacks would constitute 45 percent of the electorate, the annexation would diminish the political power of blacks and was thus ineligible for pre-clearance.[18]

The Supreme Court reversed, holding that so long as black voters were guaranteed fair representation in post-annexation Richmond in proportion to their new 45 percent status, the shift from majority to minority status was not an alteration which denied or abridged the right to vote on account of race or color. The Court noted, however, that if the purpose, as opposed to the effect, of the annexation was to reduce the power of black voters, it could not receive pre-clearance. The Court, therefore, remanded the Richmond case to the district court to determine whether reasons unrelated to race motivated the annexation of the white enclave.

Justices Douglas, Brennan and Marshall strongly dissented from the refusal to condemn the Richmond annexation on the basis of its effect upon black voters. After Richmond, it appears that pre-clearance may not be withheld merely because, as a factual matter, minority voters will be worse off after the alteration, unless the purpose of the alteration is to disadvantage minority voters. However, since purposeful election legislation designed to disadvantage racial minorities is already barred by the Fifteenth Amendment, many people fear that the Richmond decision may have weakened one of the most significant protections granted by the Voting Rights Act.

Of course, if a proposed alteration has the effect of seriously disadvantaging minority voters, pre-clearance must continue to be denied, even after Richmond. Thus, in the Richmond decision itself, the majority agreed that pre-clearance of the proposed annexation was properly denied when the proposed annexation was coupled with a shift to at-large election of councilmen, thus potentially depriving the black voters of any representation. (The impact of at-large voting on submerged racial minorities is discussed *supra*.)

After Richmond, a shift from majority to minority status does not have the "effect" of denying or abridging the right to vote, but the failure to provide blacks with fair representation within the proposed new political entity requires the denial of pre-clearance. The extent of detriment which a minority must suffer to compel a denial of pre-clearance is thus currently an unknown quantity.

What are the consequences of the failure of a covered subdivision to obtain pre-clearance?

Unless a covered subdivision secures pre-clearance, it may not enforce or administer any change or alteration in its election law. A purported alteration which has not been granted pre-clearance is void, and pre-existing election laws remain in effect. The attorney general is authorized to enjoin the enforcement of any alteration which has not received pre-clearance. Although the Voting Rights Act does not explicitly provide for private enforcement of the pre-clearance provisions, the Supreme Court ruled in *Allen* v. *State Board of Elections* [19] that any person adversely affected by the enforcement of a law subject to pre-clearance may seek an injunction against its enforcement pending pre-clearance review. Although several members of the current Supreme Court have expressed disagreement with the *Allen* decision, the reenactment of the Act by Congress in 1975 would appear to constitute congressional ratification of the private enforcement of pre-clearance. The private injunction action may be brought before a statutory three-judge court in the covered subdivision.

Only three issues are before the court in connection with such an action: (a) is the subdivision in question subject to pre-clearance; (b) does law or practice in question affect the electoral process; and (c) has pre-clearance been obtained? If the first two issues are resolved affirmatively and the third negatively, the Court must enjoin the implementation of the law in question. The merits of whether the law in question denies or abridges the right to vote on account of race, color, or membership in a language minority is not before such a court, since only the attorney general or the United States District Court for the District of Columbia is authorized to rule on the merits.

Is the imposition of a pre-clearance requirement on covered political subdivisions constitutional?

In *Katzenbach* v. *Morgan* and *South Carolina* v. *Katzenbach*,[20] the Supreme Court upheld the constitutionality of the pre-clearance provisions of the Voting Rights Act of 1965 on the ground that the Fifteenth Amendment authorized Congress to enact drastic legislation to safeguard the voting rights of racial minorities. The 1975 version of the Act, which extends pre-clearance coverage to language as well as racial minorities, cannot be sustained on purely Fifteenth Amendment grounds. However, it seems likely that the 1975 version will be sustained as an appropriate exercise of legislative power under the Equal Protection Clause of the Fourteenth Amendment.

May a covered subdivision be released from pre-clearance scrutiny?

A covered subdivision may remove itself completely from pre-clearance scrutiny by obtaining a declaratory judgment from a three-judge district court in the District of Columbia that it has not administered any "test or device" during a specified period with the purpose or effect of denying or abridging the right to vote on account of race, color, or membership in a language minority. It has proven extremely difficult to secure such a judicial exemption from pre-clearance.

What protections does the 1975 Extension of the Voting Rights Act provide for members of language minorities?

In addition to including certain political subdivisions containing substantial blocs of Spanish-speaking and Native American residents under the Act's pre-clearance provisions, the 1975 extension of the Voting Rights Act continues the ban on literacy tests in Federal, state, and local elections through 1982. Even more importantly, the 1975 extension requires subdivisions in which more than 5 percent of the eligible voters are members of language minorities to conduct bilingual election and registration campaigns.[21] The Department of Justice has been charged with the responsibility of compiling a listing of subdivisions containing the required 5 percent linguistic minority. Preliminary estimates indicate that bilingual elections will be required in Texas, California, and substantial segments of Florida, Colorado, Alaska, Arizona, and New Mexico.

Bilingual elections are required under Title III of the Voting Rights Act Amendments of 1975 in any political subdivision in which the Director of the Census certifies that 5 percent of the eligible voters are members of a language minority and that the illiteracy rate prevailing within the language minority is higher than the national average. A tentative listing of areas requiring bilingual elections is found in 40 Fed. Reg. 41827 (Sept. 9, 1975) and 43044 (September 18, 1975).

Bilingual election requirements imposed by the 1975 Voting Rights Act Amendments are in effect in the following subdivisions: Alaska (Native Alaskan); Arizona (Spanish throughout the state; American Indian in Apache, Coconino, Gila, Graham, Navajo and Pinal Counties); St. Bernard's Parish, Louisiana (Spanish); Neshoba County, Mississippi (American Indian); Texas (Spanish); Charles City County, Virginia (American Indian); Kings, Merced, Monterey and Yuba Counties, California (Spanish); El Paso, Colorado (Spanish); Hardee, Hillsborough and Monroe Counties, Florida (Spanish); Honolulu, Hawaii (Chinese & Filipino); Bronx, Kings and New York Counties, New York (Spanish); Hoke, Jackson and Robeson Counties, North Carolina (American Indian).

What protection does the Voting Rights Act provide for presidential elections?

The 1970 amendments to the Voting Rights Act of 1965 (which were reenacted in 1975 for seven years) provide that voter registration must be made available by the states in connection with presidential elections up to 30 days prior to the election. The 30-day requirement has been construed to require continuously available registration.[22] Thus, any attempt to close voter registration in a presidential year prior to 30 days before the election is in violation of the Voting Rights Act. In addition, the 1970 amendments require that convenient uniform absentee ballots be provided for presidential elections. Finally, the 1970 Act guarantees that no eligible voter can be disqualified from voting for president because he or she has moved from one state to another after the close of voter registration.

The Act provides that to the extent such an eligible voter is unable to register in her or his new residence, the voter must be permitted to vote from her or his old residence.

Two aspects of the 1970 amendments which initially appeared of great significance have been mooted by subsequent events. The lowering of the voting age to 18 was superseded by the Twenty-sixth Amendment, and the abolition of durational residence requirement for voting in presidential elections was rendered obsolete by the Supreme Court's total abolition of durational residence requirements for voting in *Dunn* v. *Blumstein,* discussed *supra* in Chapter II.

The constitutionality of the 1970 amendments was sustained by a seriously fragmented Supreme Court with the significant exception of the Act's attempt to lower the voting age in state and local (as opposed to Federal) elections to 18 years of age.[23]

Has there been any legislative attempt to reform the registration process?

Yes. New York State has recently enacted the nation's first mail-registration system.[24] Many political scientists believe that the key to improving voter participation lies not so much in striking down overtly illegal election processes, but rather in making voter registration more conveniently available. Most Western democracies place the burden of registering eligible voters on the government. In the United States, however, at least since the turn of the century, the onus of registering to vote has been borne solely by the individual voters. Registration is often not conveniently available and must take place long before the election. Although courts have imposed some limitation on onerous registration practices, broad legislative reform seems a precondition to major improvement. New York's law is based upon a proposed Federal mail-registration statute which has been perennially considered—but never passed—by Congress.

The Voting Rights Act permits a Federal court or the Attorney General to supersede local registration machinery with Federal voting registrars upon a showing that it operates in a racially discriminatory manner. While Federal registrars have played constructive roles in certain elections, they have not been widely utilized. Federal poll watchers have been resorted to with much greater frequency.

NOTES

1. Kramer v. Union Free School District No. 15, 395 U.S. 621 (1969).
2. Pope v. Williams, 193 U.S. 621 (1904).
3. The Voting Rights Act, as amended, is set forth at 42 U.S.C. §§1973 et. seq., as amended 85 Stat 315 (1970) and 89 Stat. 400 (1975).
4. See generally, Section 5 of the Voting Rights Act of 1965, 42 U.S.C. §1973(c).
5. Section 4(c) of the Voting Rights Act of 1965, 42 U.S.C. §1973 b.
6. Section 4(f)(3) of the Voting Rights Act Amendments of 1975, 42 U.S.C. 1973 b.
7. Allen v. State Board of Elections, 393 U.S. 544 (1969); Perkins v. Matthews, 400 U.S. 379 (1971) on remand, 336 F. Supp. 6 (S.D. Miss. 1971); Georgia v. United States, 411 U.S. 526 (1973).
8. See generally, New York v. United States, 419 U.S. (1974).
9. United Jewish Org. of Williamsburgh v. Wilson, 510 F2d 512 (2d Cir. 1975) cert. granted, ——— U.S. ——— (1975).
10. Connor v. Johnson, 402 U.S. 690 (1971).
11. The regulations governing the processing and disposition of pre-clearance submissions by the Justice Department are set forth at Title 28 C.F.R. Part 51 (1971).

12. City of Richmond v. United States, 376 F.Supp. 1344 (D.D.C. 1974) rev'd. 95 S.Ct. 2296 (1975).
13. Evers v. State Board of Elections, 327 F.Supp. 640 (S.D. Miss. 1971).
14. Common Cause v. Mitchell, Civ. No. 2348-71 (D.D.C. March 30, 1972).
15. Section 5 of the Voting Rights Act of 1965, 42 U.S.C. §1973.
16. 28 C.F.R. §51.19 (1971).
17. Georgia v. United States, 411 U.S. 526 (1973).
18. City of Richmond v. United States, 376 F.Supp. 1344 (D.D.C. 1974) rev'd, 95 S.Ct. 2296 (1975).
19. Allen v. State Board of Elections, 393 U.S. 544 (1969).
20. Katzenbach v. Morgan, 384 U.S. 641 (1966); South Carolina v. Katzenbach, 383 U.S. 301 (1966).
21. Title III of the Voting Rights Act Amendments of 1975, 42 U.S.C. §1973.
22. Bishop v. Lomenzo, 350 F.Supp. 576 (E.D.N.Y. 1972).
23. Oregon v. Mitchell, 400 U.S. 112 (1970).
24. New York Election Law, §153.

VII

Legislative Reform of the Financing and Conduct of Election Campaigns

Why have legislators become increasingly concerned with reforming the campaign process?

Traditionally, the phenomenon that is the American political campaign has operated on a virtually unregulated basis. However, as campaigning became an enormously expensive process, fears that monied interests were exercising a disproportionate influence on political life in America, in return for financing candidates, became widespread. In response to that fear—and to the pervasive cynicism and mistrust of government which it engendered—legislators have become increasingly concerned with reforming the means by which American political campaigns are financed. In addition, moved by the revelation of widespread "dirty tricks" in connection with the 1972 presidential campaign, legislators have sought to impose controls on unfair campaign practices. Whether such reforms—well-meaning as they are—violate fundamental constitutional guarantees of freedom of speech and association; unduly benefit incumbents and majority parties; and endanger the democratic process by intimately involving the government in the conduct of political campaigns, remains a hotly debated issue.

The clash between reforming zeal and constitutional values culminated in the Supreme Court in *Buckley* v. *Valeo*, ——— U.S. ——— (1975)[1] in which large segments of the Federal Election Campaign Act of 1974 were invalidated, while other critical reforms were upheld. Whether the surviving provisions can stand alone remains problematical. In this chapter we will set out the reforms which the 1974 Act attempted and explore whether they survived the Court's constitutional scrutiny.

What was wrong with our existing methods of campaign financing?

Our piecemeal and fragmented attempts to regulate campaign financing proved inadequate to prevent special interests from funneling enormous sums into political campaigns.

In 1907[2] Congress passed the first campaign financing legislation forbidding national banks and congressionally chartered corporations from contributing to federal election campaigns. In 1910 Congress required those political committees operating in congressional elections in two or more states to disclose all transactions in excess of $100. Similarly, expenditures of $50, made independently of such a political committee had to be disclosed. In 1911 the legislation was broadened to establish for the first time, overall expenditure ceilings on campaigns for the House and for the Senate. The 1911 revision also broadened disclosure to include the primary, convention, and prenomination expenditures. In 1918 Congress made it a crime to offer money to influence voting. In 1925 Congress codified preexisting law in the Federal Corrupt Practices Act of 1925, which served as the primary regulation of campaign financing until the recent reforms. In 1939 Congress enacted the Hatch Act, which bans overt political activities by Federal employees. (The Hatch Act is discussed, *infra*.) In 1940 Congress imposed an annual expenditure ceiling of $3,000,000 on any political committee and limited endurance contributions to candidates or political committees to $5,000 in any calendar year. Since no limit on the creation and number of political committees existed, the 1940 Act was neatly evaded by the simple expedient of multiplying political committees. Thus, if a wealthy contributor wished to avoid the $5,000 ceiling, he was able to donate $5,000 to a candidate and $5,000 to an endless parade of political committees established on the candidate's behalf. Moreover, by dividing his contribution among an infinite number of committees, the total gift to each often fell below the disclosure minimum. In 1943 and 1947 Congress extended the ban on corporate contributions and imposed a prohibition on contributions by labor unions as well. In 1966 Congress enacted a short-lived $1 tax checkoff plan to permit public financing of presidential elections, but it was effectively repealed in 1967. In 1971 Congress revived the $1 tax checkoff and enacted the Federal Elections Campaign Act of 1971, requiring disclosure of all political contributions in excess of $100 and detailed disclosure of expenditures by most Federal candidates. Finally, in 1974, Congress enacted the comprehensive amendments to the F.E.C.A. providing for broad disclosure, enforceable contribution and expenditive ceilings, public financing of presidential primaries, conventions, and elections, and the creation of a full-time administrative agency to enforce the Act. It was the 1974 version of the Federal Elections Campaign Act which was before the Supreme Court in *Buckley* v. *Valeo*.[3]

One incident in connection with the 1972 presidential campaign illustrates why the piecemeal legislation which preceded the 1974 amendments was ineffective. During 1970, representatives of the nation's dairy industry were concerned that price supports to dairy farmers were too low. Intensive lobbying with the Secretary of Agriculture failed to achieve a rise in the supports. The dairy interests then turned their attention to President Nixon, pledging $2,000,000 to his 1972 presidential campaign. Of course, a contribution of that size from a corporation or group of corporations was flatly prohibited by existing law. Instead, in November 1970, the milk producers offered to donate the money in $2,500 payments to hundreds of political committees in various states to be held for the 1972 campaign. Such a device permitted them to donate the money in such small payments that no disclosure would be required and, at the same time, enabled them to avoid the $5,000 contribution ceiling which had been imposed in 1940. On March 23, 1971, after a meeting between President Nixon and the dairy industry leaders, President Nixon promised an increase in milk price supports, but before his decision was publicly announced, the dairymen were required to reaffirm the $2,000,000 pledge. It is, of course, immaterial whether President Nixon's decision was linked to the contributions. The appearance of undue influence is so palpable that public confidence in the integrity of the decision-making process could not survive unless reforms were enacted. Of course, whether the 1974 reforms create a greater danger of interference with free elections than the evil they were designed to combat is the serious question which confronted the Supreme Court in *Buckley* v. *Valeo*.

How did the 1974 Act seek to reform campaign financing?

The 1974 Act attempted to reform campaign financing by imposing four interrelated sets of controls. First, the Act imposes stringent ceilings on the amounts which can be contributed to or expended by or on behalf of a candidate; second, the Act requires public disclosure of any substantial campaign contribution; third, the Act provides for public subsidies for the presidential nomination and election process; and, finally, the Act establishes a permanent agency to monitor compliance with its terms.

Does the 1974 Act purport to regulate all elections?
No. The Federal Act regulates only presidential, senatorial and congressional elections. Campaigns for state offices are not covered by the Act. However, many states and localities have enacted similar legislation imposing spending limits on local elections.

How much may a "person" contribute to a single candidate for President, the Senate or the House of Representatives?
Under the 1974 Act, a person (meaning an individual, partnership, committee, association, or other organization or group) may contribute up to $1,000 to a candidate for Federal office in connection with each election in which the candidate is involved. The old practice of evading the law by proliferating dummy committees to receive contributions is precluded, since all gifts to any entity under the direction and control of the candidate are treated as gifts to the candidate for the purpose of calculating the $1,000 ceiling. As originally drafted, contributions to entities outside the candidate's direction and control did not count toward the $1,000, but if they were designed to advance or retard the candidacy of a particular identified candidate, such independent gifts were subject to a second $1,000 ceiling.

In *Buckley* v. *Valeo,* the Supreme Court upheld the $1,000 contribution ceiling for contributions to a candidate or to anyone under the candidate's direction or control. A majority of the Court ruled that, while political contributions were related to free speech, the government was authorized to impose contribution maximums in order to safeguard the integrity of the electoral process. The majority distinguished between contributions (which they held can be regulated) and individual expenditures on behalf of a candidate (which they held exempt from regulation), on the ground that expenditures involve "direct" communicative activity while contributions involve a more "indirect" communication. The dissenters argued that both contributions and individual expenditures should be treated equally, with several Justices arguing that each was exempt from regulation and Justice White arguing that both were subject to regulation. Whether the uneasy compromise which the majority endorsed, involving an analytically questionable distinction between contributions to a candidate and expenditures on behalf of a candidate, will withstand the test of time is problematical. Under current law, however, a voter is limited to a $1,000 contribution to a candidate but may personally expend an unlimited amount on behalf of the candidate as long as the expenditure is not under the candidate's direction and control. In the wake of *Buckley* v. *Valeo,* a dispute has arisen concerning campaign gifts to independent entities which are not under the candidate's direction and control, but which are working for his or her election. As the 1974 law was originally drafted, gifts to independent political committees were subject to a $1,000 ceiling. However, after *Buckley,* it is unclear whether such gifts are "individual expenditures" and, therefore, exempt from any ceiling, or "contributions" and, thus, subject to the $1,000 ceiling. The difficulty inherent in resolving the ambiguity points up the weakness in the Supreme Court's analysis.

For the purposes of the $1,000 contribution ceiling,

primaries, runoffs, and general elections are treated as separate elections, except that all the presidential primaries are lumped together and treated as a single election for the purposes of computing contribution ceilings. Thus, if an individual wishes to support a favored candidate, he or she may contribute up to $1,000 toward the campaign expenses of a primary election and an additional $1,000 toward the general election campaign. If either the primary or the general election requires a separate runoff, an individual would be permitted to contribute an additional $1,000 in connection with it. In supporting a favored presidential candidate, a contributor may give no more than $1,000 toward the candidate's total primary expenses, regardless of how many primaries are entered, and an additional $1,000 toward the general election.

How much may an individual contribute to all candidates for Federal office in any calendar year?

The Act places a ceiling of $25,000 on the amount which any individual may contribute to candidates for Federal office in any calendar year. For the purpose of the $25,000 ceiling, contributions made in connection with a given election campaign period are deemed to have been made in the calendar year in which the general election takes place. Contributions to a vice-presidential candidate are attributed to his or her running mate for the purpose of calculating contribution ceilings.

In *Buckley,* the Supreme Court upheld the $25,000 annual ceiling on all Federal campaign contributions. However, after *Buckley,* no limits exist on the amount which an individual may personally expend on behalf of candidates. Once again, it is unclear whether gifts to independent entities not under the candidate's direction and control fall under or count toward the $25,000 ceiling. If they are deemed contributions, they are subject to the ceiling; if they are deemed expenditures, they are not subject to the ceiling.

How much cash may a person contribute to a political campaign for Federal office?

Total cash contributions to candidates for Federal office in excess of $100 in any calendar year are prohibited.

What constitutes a contribution within the meaning of the Act?

Obviously, gifts of money or property are deemed contributions. In addition, loans to candidates are deemed contributions, with the exception of loans made by banks in the ordinary course of business. Even bank loans may be deemed contributions if the loan is endorsed or guaranteed by a third person, in which case the loan is treated as a contribution from the endorser or guarantor to the candidate. To the extent that an individual pays the salary of persons providing services to a candidate, he or she is deemed to be making a contribution. Finally, a promise to make a future contribution—whether or not legally enforceable—is treated as a current contribution.[4]

The value of services rendered to candidates by volunteers, generally, is not a contribution.[5] Thus, for example, volunteers may expend unlimited time and energy regardless of the fair market value of their services without being deemed to have made a contribution to a favored candidate. Moreover, individuals who volunteer their homes for campaign activities and expend personal funds up to $500 for invitations, food, and beverages are not deemed to make a contribution. Food or beverage vendors who provide merchandise at cost do not make a contribution as long as the lost profit does not exceed $500; but other suppliers who provide materials at less than fair market value will be deemed to have made a contribution of their lost profits. Finally, volunteers who incur unreimbursed travel expenses of up to $500 do not make a contribution. The preparation of slate cards or sample ballots and their distribution by a state or local party committee is not a contribution, so long as the slate cards list at least three candidates. News stories, editorials, and commentaries by the press and broadcast media are not deemed contributions.

Who is a candidate within the meaning of the 1974 Act?

The 1974 Act defines a candidate as an individual who has taken action to qualify under the law of any state for nomination or election to the office in question *or* who has received contributions or received expenditures or given consent to any other person to do so with a view toward bringing about nomination or election.[6]

Does the 1974 Act place controls on contributions or expenditures involving issues rather than specified candidates?

No. The Act's provisions apply only to gifts to or on behalf of candidates in Federal elections. The regulations have no application to contributions or expenditures designed to advance a point of view on public issues—including campaign issues—so long as the gift does not have the primary purpose of advocating the election or defeat of a clearly identified candidate. Thus, even under the Act as originally drafted, persons were permitted to spend unlimited sums on public issues, so long as they did not involve the advocacy of a specific, clearly identified candidate.[7]

How are there any limits on the amounts which an

individual can spend personally to bring about the election of a specific candidate?

As originally drafted, the 1974 Act imposed a $1,000 ceiling on the amount which an individual voter could spend to advocate the election of a specified candidate. The imposition of such an individual expenditure limit was one of the Act's most controversial provisions. Under its terms, a citizen was not permitted to purchase a full-page advertisement advocating a favored candidate if the cost of the advertisement exceeded $1,000. In *Buckley,* the Supreme Court invalidated individual expenditure limitations as a "direct" interference with free speech. Thus, under current law, there are no limits on the amount which an individual may personally expend advocating the election of a specified candidate. However, when an individual makes a gift to a group which is not under the direction and control of a candidate, but which exists to further the interest of a specified candidate, it is unclear whether such a gift is an exempt expenditure or a controlled contribution.

What is a political committee?

The 1974 Act defines a "political committee" as "any committee, club, association, or other group of persons which receives contributions or makes expenditures during a calendar year in an aggregate amount exceeding $1,000." [8] So defined, it encompasses virtually every entity which can be active in financing or administering a political campaign. Political committees must consist of at least six persons and register with the Federal Election Commission. Six months after registration, political committees may contribute up to $5,000 to a candidate. However, after *Buckley,* no limits may be placed on the "expenditures," as opposed to the "contributions" of a political committee. The 6-month waiting period is designated to prevent individuals (who are subject to a $1,000 ceiling) from forming an *ad hoc* committee which would have a $5,000 ceiling. The voluntary funds collected by corporations and labor unions are treated as political committees.

May corporations or labor unions contribute to Federal election compaigns?

Not directly. The long-standing ban on contributions by corporations and labor unions has been continued by the Act.[9] However, the Act permits both corporations and labor unions to establish segregated funds into which voluntary contributions may flow and from which political contributions may be made. The $5,000 ceiling on expenditures by a political committee to or on behalf of a particular candidate applies to a corporate or labor union voluntary fund. After *Buckley,* a corporate or labor voluntary fund may expend unlimited amounts on behalf of a candidate so long as the funds are not controlled by the candidate. Thus, under current law, such corporate or labor committees wield enormous power—especially if gifts to them are deemed personal expenditures rather than contributions. State bans on corporate contributions have occasionally been narrowly construed. One Federal court construed New York's ban on corporate contributions to apply only to partisan election campaigns, thus permitting corporations to expend money to influence referenda in which they were interested.[10] The Supreme Court has ruled that enforcement of the Federal ban on corporate contributions is the sole responsibility of the Attorney General and the Federal Election Commission. The Court rejected the argument that the Federal Act grants an implied private cause of action to shareholders to recover illegal corporate contributions.[11]

Finally, the 1974 Act imposes a flat ban on political

contributions by foreign nationals and government con-
tractors.[12]

How much may a candidate's family contribute?

The 1974 Act provided stringent ceilings on contributions by a candidate or his immediate family to the
campaign. Candidates for president were permitted to
expend $50,000 in personal or immediate family funds
in any calendar year; candidates for the Senate were
limited to $35,000; and congressional candidates were
permitted to expend $25,000 of their own funds dur-
ing the campaign. All outstanding intrafamily loans
and advances were permitted to be computed in calculating the ceiling. A candidate's family included
his or her spouse, children, parents, grandparents,
brothers, sisters, and their respective spouses. Uncles
and other collateral relatives were subject to the
$1,000 ceiling which governs the public at large. In-
trafamily contributors were each subject to the $25,000
ceiling on aggregate individual contributions.[13] In
Buckley, the Supreme Court invalidated all ceilings on
the use of personal funds by a candidate. Thus, a
wealthy candidate may spend an unlimited amount on
his or her candidacy. The Court left intact, however,
the restrictions on contributions to a candidate by
close family members. Thus, after *Buckley,* a candidate
may spend unlimited personal funds, but may not receive contributions from close family members in excess of the $1,000 per person ceiling. Of course, close
family members may, apparently, expend unlimited
funds on behalf of a candidate, so long as the expenditures are not under the candidate's direction and control.

May a candidate accept honoraria as a method of raising funds?

The 1974 Act halts the time-honored practice of

supplementing congressional income by lecture tours by forbidding any elective or appointive officer of the Federal government from accepting any honorarium in excess of $1,000, or aggregate honoraria of more than $15,000 in any calendar year, "for any appearance, speech, or article."

How much may a presidential candidate expend on the primary campaign?

Under the original Act, candidates in presidential primaries were limited to an aggregate total expenditure of $10,000,000.[14] Within each state, a presidential primary candidate was limited to twice that which a Senate primary candidate would be permitted to spend. If a candidate were seeking two offices in a given state simultaneously—such as a Senate nomination and the presidency—he or she was limited to the expenditure ceiling placed on the lower office. Thus, in simultaneously seeking the presidential nomination and nomination to the Senate from Texas, Lloyd Bentsen's Texas expenditures for both the presidential and the Senate races were limited by the senatorial ceiling.

In *Buckley,* the Supreme Court invalidated all expenditure ceilings on spending of candidates. Thus, a candidate may now spend as much as he or she can raise. However, the Court ruled that it was constitutional to require those candidates accepting Federal campaign subsidies to promise to limit their expenditures to the maximum set by the Act. Thus, a candidate may forego Federal campaign subsidies and spend as much money as he or she can raise—remembering that individual contributions continue to be limited to $1,000; or a candidate may accept Federal subsidy and, thereby, place an expenditure ceiling on his or her campaign. Of course, the acceptance of Federal funding (and the concomitant expenditure ceiling) in no way inhibits a candidate's supporters from spending unlimited sums on his election, so long as the expenditures are not subject to the candidate's control.

How much may a senatorial candidate spend on the primary campaign?

Persons seeking a senatorial nomination in a primary may spend $100,000, or 8 cents per resident of voting age in the state, whichever is higher. In the general election, 12 cents per eligible voter may be spent.[15]

Since the law provides no public funding for Congressional or Senatorial elections, the Supreme Court's decision removes all restraints on expenditures in House or Senate elections.

How much may a House candidate spend on the primary campaign?

In House races in those states which are entitled to only one representative, the Senate limits apply. When two or more representatives may be elected from a state, each candidate may spend $70,000 on the primary and $70,000 on the general election.[16]

Since the law provides no public funding for Congressional or Senatorial elections, the Supreme Court's decision removes all restraints on expenditures in House or Senate elections.

How much may a candidate for the presidency spend on the general election?

The Act imposes a ceiling of $20,000,000 in connection with a general election for the presidency, all of which comes from public funds.[17] If the public subsidy is accepted, the expenditure ceiling is effective.

Are sums expended in fund raising counted as campaign expenditures?

Not entirely. Candidates are permitted to spend up to 20 percent of their expenditure ceiling for the purpose of soliciting contributions without having such disbursements considered as expenditures subject to the ceiling.

Are independent expenditures by supporters on his behalf counted toward the candidate's expenditure ceiling?

No. The unlimited sum which an individual is permitted to expend independently to advance the election of a favored candidate does not count in computing the candidate's expenditure ceiling. Thus, a candidate may accept public subsidy, and thus, place a ceiling on his campaign expenditures, but continue to receive the benefit of unlimited expenditures by his supporters.

Once a candidate has reached the expenditure ceiling, must spending cease?

Not necessarily. Even if a candidate has elected to receive public funds, and, thus, placed himself under an expenditure ceiling, in addition to the contribution and expenditure ceilings, the national committee of a political party and a state committee (or its geographical subdivisions) may make expenditures on behalf of an affiliated candidate for Federal office as follows:

1. For president—2 cents per voting-age resident of the United States. Current population figures would authorize an additional expenditure of $2,800,000.
2. For senator: 2 cents per voting age residents of the state or $20,000, whichever is greater.
3. For representatives: $10,000.

Must a candidate decline contributions which would exceed his or her expenditure ceiling?

Not necessarily. While the excess contributions may not be expended on the campaign, the Act permits excess contributions to be used to defray the expenses of carrying out the duties of an elected office; to be given away to charity; or to be used "for any other lawful purpose." Excess campaign funds may not be utilized for the personal benefit of a candidate unless they are declared as ordinary income for tax purposes.

Are the expenditure ceilings for candidates and national and state party committees fixed?

No. The expenditure and contribution ceilings established by the 1974 Act are in effect only during 1975. Commencing in 1976, the 1975 ceilings must be adjusted upward to keep pace with rises in the Consumer Price Index, as published annually by the Department of Labor. Interestingly, the Act does not even comprehend the possibility of a decrease in the Consumer Price Index.[18]

How much may a political party spend on its national convention?

The Act limits spending by both major and minor parties in connection with national conventions to $2,000,000, with the ceiling subject to future upward adjustment in accordance with the Consumer Price Index. The Federal Election Commission may authorize additional emergency expenditures due to "extraordinary and unforeseen circumstances." If the Federal subsidy for conventions is accepted, the ceiling remains effective. If, however, a party foregoes public subsidy, it may spend unlimited sums on its convention. Contributions to a party to defray convention expenses are not subject to a ceiling, since they are not contributions to a specified candidate.

How does the 1974 Act ensure disclosure of the identities of campaign contributors?

First, the Act outlaws aggregate cash contributions of more than $100 by any individual.

Second, the Act requires all candidates and political committees to record all contributions, no matter how small.

Third, candidates and political committees must record the identity of every person contributing more than an aggregate of $10. Although such information need not be made public, it must be made available to the Federal Election Commission for audit purposes.

Fourth, candidates and political committees must keep a public record of the names, occupations, and principal places of business of all persons contributing more than $100 and all persons to whom funds are paid.[19]

Thus, to insure anonymity, a contributor to a candidate for Federal office must give less than $10. Gifts in excess of $100 ensure public disclosure. Gifts of from $10 to $100 are known to the staff of the Federal Elections Commission, but not necessarily to the general public.

Must contributions to public-issue organizations be disclosed?

As originally drafted, the 1974 Act required public disclosure of contributors to issue-oriented organizations like the NAACP or the ACLU, if those organizations took positions on public issues during the campaign. However, such overbroad disclosure provisions were declared unconstitutional even before *Buckley* v. *Valeo*. Thus, gifts to a public-issue organization whose primary purpose is not the influence of a given election now fall outside the disclosure provisions of the Act.

Must independent expenditures on behalf of a candidate be publicly reported?

Yes. Although the Supreme Court invalidated independent expenditure ceilings, the Court upheld the disclosure requirement. Thus, if a person expends funds on behalf of a candidate, he or she must publicly disclose the expenditure if it exceeds $100. If a person purchases a mimeograph machine and prints leaflets on behalf of a candidate, he must publicly disclose his activity if his expenditures exceed $100.

Must expenditures designed to influence decisions on "issues" rather than "candidates" be disclosed?

No. The Supreme Court construed the 1974 Act narrowly to require disclosure only when an expenditure or contribution advocates a specific candidate. Issue-oriented expenditures and contributions need not be publicly disclosed, even if they deal with hotly contested campaign issues.[20]

Must contributions and expenditures on behalf of minority party candidates be disclosed?

As an initial matter, yes. Thus, a gift of more than $10 to a controversial political candidate must be reported by the candidate to the Federal Elections Commission, and if the gift exceeds $100, it must be publicly recorded. However, in upholding the constitutionality of such minority party disclosure, the Supreme Court ruled that any party or individual may gain an exemption from disclosure by demonstrating a threat of harassment because of unpopular political views. Only a court may grant such an exemption and, although the Supreme Court guidelines do not appear onerous, the expense and difficulty of Federal litigation will doubtless render such exemptions difficult to obtain as a practical matter.

Does the act provide for government subsidies for all Federal elections?

No. While the expenditure and contribution ceilings and the disclosure requirements apply to all Federal officials, the public-funding provisions apply only to presidential elections.

How does the public subsidy of presidential elections work?

The Act creates the Presidential Election Campaign Fund, consisting of monies allocated by a voluntary tax checkoff system which permits taxpayers to allocate $1 or $2 to the fund. Unlike earlier proposals, the current checkoff system does not permit a taxpayer to designate a party or candidate. The fund is disbursed to presidential candidates in three stages: presidential primaries; nominating conventions; and the general election. To the extent that the fund is insufficient, it must be expended, first, to subsidize the national conventions; second, to subsidize the general election; and, if sums remain, the primary races.[21]

How are the subsidies to be allocated?

The Act divides political parties into three groups.[22] Parties which received at least 25 percent of the popular vote in the last presidential election are deemed "major" parties; parties receiving between 5 percent and 25 percent are deemed "minor" parties; while parties garnering less than 5 percent are deemed "new" parties. Major parties receive the lion's share of the subsidy, while "minor" parties receive only a proportionate payment based upon their most recent presidential showing. "New" parties receive nothing until after the election, and then only if they poll 5 percent of the popular vote. At the present time, only candidates of the Republican and Democratic parties qualify for presidential subsidies. In the twentieth century, only three nonmajor party candidates for president have ever secured 5 percent of the popular vote: Theodore Roosevelt (1912—Progressive Party), Eugene Debs (1912—Socialist Party) twice, and Robert Lafollette (1924—Progressive Party).

The allocation of the subsidy has been criticized as unfair, first, because it is based upon figures from the last presidential election, and thus does not reflect current relative party strength; and second, because it provides severely limited funds to "minor" parties and no funds at all for "new" parties during the campaign itself, while providing comfortable subsidies to the established parties during the critical campaign period. Critics of the law argue that "new" and often controversial parties are triply hurt by the Act, first, by being denied any subsidy during the campaign; second, by being denied access to private funding because of being subjected to the same $1,000 individual contribution ceiling imposed on major parties; and third, by forced public disclosure of even its modest supporters. Certainly the unfair advantage enjoyed by the major parties in the form of exclusive subsidies and the serious disadvantage imposed upon "new" parties (such as the Communists, Socialists, Progressives, and American Labor parties) by impeding their access to private funds, raises serious constitutional questions. In *Buckley,* the Supreme Court upheld the constitutionality of the allocation of campaign subsidies to the established parties. A majority of the Court held that since a major party candidate, by accepting public subsidy also accepts expenditure ceilings, an indirect benefit accrued to minority candidates who, free from the "burden" of a public subsidy, were free to raise privately (subject to the $1,000 contribution ceiling and the $10 disclosure requirement) and expend unlimited funds. Such a possibility must give cold comfort to an under-funded minority party.

How are the national conventions subsidized?

Major parties receive a flat grant of $2,000,000, adjusted by the Consumer Price Index, to operate their national convention.[23] The grant must be paid by July 1 of the year preceding the convention. Thus, on July 1, 1975, the Republican and Democratic parties each received $2,000,000 to finance the 1976 conventions in New York City and Kansas City. Since many expenses of a convention are assumed by the host city in the form of a rent-free convention hall and related inducements, and since delegates traditionally pay their own way, the $2,000,000 grant appears ample. Since no "minor" parties exist, no other payments were made to subsidize other 1976 conventions. If, by some quirk, a "new" party survives the discriminatory aspects of the Act and receives 5 percent of the vote in 1976, it will not qualify for a retroactive convention subsidy, since no retroactive convention subsidies are authorized. Thus, if a new party secures 10 percent of the popular vote in the 1976 presidential election, it will not qualify for a retroactive convention subsidy. However, in 1980, it would be entitled to its pro rata convention subsidy in advance. In *Buckley,* the Supreme Court upheld the convention subsidy plan.

How are the presidential general election campaigns subsidized?

Upon nomination, the presidential candidate of a major party receives a flat grant of $20,000,000 to subsidize his or her campaign.[24] In return for receiving the public funds, the candidate must make available all records to the Federal Election Commission for ongoing audit, must refrain from seeking private funds unless public funds become unavailable, and must refrain from expenditures in excess of the $20,000,000 ceiling.[25] The presidential candidates of "minor" parties would be entitled to a grant upon nomination determined by the party's proportionate showing in the last presidential election. Thus, if a "minor" party captures 5 percent of the vote in 1976, in 1980 it would be entitled to a $1,000,000 campaign subsidy. If, despite receiving no campaign subsidy, a new party secures more than 5 percent of the vote in the general election, it is entitled to a retroactive payment of its proportionate subsidy. Thus, although no new party qualifies for a campaign subsidy in connection with the 1976 election, if a new party polls 10 percent of the vote, it will retroactively receive 15 cents for each vote.[26]

May independent candidates who are not affiliated with any party qualify for a presidential subsidy?

The subsidy provisions of the 1974 Act are phrased solely in terms of political parties. Thus, read literally, an independent candidate for president is ineligible for a campaign subsidy. However, such a result would almost certainly be struck down as unconstitutional. Should an independent ever qualify for subsidy, it is probable that he or she would receive it. Of course, the 5 percent hurdle must be overcome for an independent to qualify.

How are the presidential primary campaigns subsidized?

Since the number of good-faith candidates at the primary stage is substantial, the qualification for and administration of the primary subsidy is quite complex.[27]

In order to qualify for a primary subsidy, a presidential hopeful must demonstrate a substantial base of support by privately raising $100,000: securing at least

$5,000 in 20 states, with no contribution exceeding $250.[28] Once a candidate has qualified, he or she is eligible to receive matching funds from the Presidential Election Fund on a dollar-for-dollar basis for all future private contributions of up to $250. Thus, although an individual is free to contribute up to $1,000 to a presidential primary campaign, only the first $250 will be matched with public funds.[29] In determining whether the qualification figure has been reached, the gross receipts of a candidate may be utilized, without subtracting the cost of the fund-raising solicitation. Thus, even if it costs $5,000 to raise the required $5,000 in a given state, the gross $5,000 figure will be accepted for subsidy qualification purposes. Once the qualification figure has been reached, only the net receipts of a candidate should qualify for matching. Thus, if, after qualification, a candidate raises $5,000 in $250 gifts through a direct-mail solicitation which costs $2,500, only the net figure ($2,500) should qualify for Federal subsidy.

What is the Federal Election Commission and how does it operate?

The 1974 Act creates, for the first time, a full-time agency, the 8-member Federal Election Commission, empowered and authorized to enforce the Act.[30] The Secretary of the Senate and the Clerk of the House are ex-officio nonvoting members of the commission. Of the 6 voting members, 2 are appointed by the Senate, 2 by the House, and 2 by the president. No more than 3 voting members of the commission may be members of the same political party. All nominees serve a 6-year staggered term and are subject to confirmation by Congress. The four congressional appointees are actually nominated by the majority and minority leaders of the respective Houses of Congress. In addition to the members of the commission, a general counsel and substantial supporting staff is authorized.

Included among the commission's major responsibilities are rulemaking, subpoena power, power to require submission of written reports, power to conduct investigations and hearings, power to commence civil actions to enforce the Act, power to request the attorney general to enforce the Act civilly and to commence certain criminal prosecutions, and a critically important power to issue expeditious advisory opinions on disputed issues concerning candidates' and contributors' rights and responsibilities under the Act. Thus, if an ambiguity arises during a campaign, the commission may issue an advisory opinion clarifying it. Examples of commission advisory opinions include allocation of expenditures between President Ford and Louis Wyman in connection with the president's unsuccessful campaign trip to New Hampshire on Wyman's behalf. The commission ruled that the expense of the trip should be allocated to Wyman's campaign, despite the fact that the trip would be of help to the President in the forthcoming New Hampshire presidential primary.

An additional example of an ambiguous situation which required advisory clarification was Lloyd Bentsen's simultaneous campaign for the Senate and the presidency. The commission ruled that as long as Bentsen remained a candidate for the Senate, his Texas expenditures were limited to the Senate, rather then the presidential, ceiling to avoid unfairness to his Senate opponents. Finally, the commission has issued advisory opinions on whether gross or net receipts must be computed for the purposes of subsidy qualification and matching. The advisory rulings of the commission are subject to prompt judicial review and may be overruled by either House of Congress.

In addition to its general powers, the commission is specifically authorized to permit supplemental convention expenditures above the $2,000,000 ceiling and to impose a temporary disqualification on any candidate for Federal office who fails to file reports of receipts and expenditures. In *Buckley,* the Supreme Court invalidated the Federal Elections Commission, holding that since four of its members were legislative appointees, it could not exercise executive functions— such as commencing civil actions to enforce the Act or issuing regulations—without violating the principle of separation of power. The Court gave Congress fifty days to correct the deficiency.

A person who receives a favorable advisory opinion from the commission is virtually insulated against subsequent prosecution under the Act, since a person acting in good-faith reliance upon an advisory opinion is "presumed to be in compliance" with the Act.

What are the penalties for violating the 1974 Act?

Willful violation of the expenditure and contribution limits, the disclosure requirements, and the reporting aspects of the Act carry criminal penalties enforceable by the attorney general with the advice of the commission. In addition, the commission and the attorney general may commence civil actions to enjoin violations of the Act and to recover excess expenditures and contributions. Finally, the commission may impose a disqualification on a candidate who fails to file reports. The constitutionality of the disqualification sanction has not been tested.

Doesn't the 1974 Act raise serious constitutional questions?

Certainly. Any attempt to regulate the electoral

process gets perilously close to core constitutional values of freedom of speech and association which have traditionally insulated political activity from governmental regulation. Whether the 1974 Act in its reformist zeal unduly restricts free speech and association is a matter of vigorous disagreement. The New York Civil Liberties Union, the American Conservative Union, Senator James Buckley and Eugene McCarthy have all attacked the 1974 Act as an unconstitutional governmental intrusion into the political system. However, the leadership of the major parties and reform-minded organizations such as Common Cause have hailed the Act as a necessary antidote for the domination of the American political scene by monied special interests. As *Buckley* v. *Valeo* held, both the opponents and adherents of the Act were partially correct.

What are the constitutional questions raised by the Act?

Opponents of the Act levelled a number of constitutional challenges against the Act.

First, opponents assert that the expenditure and contribution ceilings imposed by the Act impinge upon freedom of speech. They argue that the contribution or expenditure of funds in pursuit of a political end is core First Amendment activity which cannot be interfered with by the government. In addition, they argue that expenditure and contribution ceilings inevitably aid incumbents, since the visibility of an incumbent and the value of his or her office as a platform and source of power inevitably places a challenger at a disadvantage which can be overcome only by outspending the incumbent.

Defenders of the Act counter by arguing that the expenditure of large sums of money to influence an election is not "pure speech" at all, but really a form of "action" which can be subjected to appropriate governmental regulation to further a compelling governmental interest in honest and fair elections. Moreover, supporters of the Act argue that the effect of the ceilings will be to enhance First Amendment values by ensuring that citizens have greater equality in expressing their political preferences. In response to the charge that expenditure and contribution ceilings favor incumbents, supporters of the Act argue that the fluidity of American political life does not support such an inference and that the levels of spending available to challengers under the Act more than permit them to reach the electorate.

In *Buckley,* the Supreme Court accepted the challengers' contentions when expenditures (by a candidate or a voter) are involved; however, the Court agreed with the Act's proponents when contributions to a specific candidate are involved.

Second, opponents of the Act charge that the disclosure provisions of the Act destroy the time-honored right to anonymity in political association and will render it virtually impossible for controversial minor parties to secure contributions. They argue that by requiring records of the identities of all donors in excess of $10 and by insuring public disclosure of all donations in excess of $100, the Act invades the right of Americans to privacy in their political beliefs and associations.

Defenders of the Act argue that, while privacy is significant value, it ought not to shield substantial contributors from public knowledge. The use of personal wealth to influence an election, they argue, is not the type of private activity which freedom of association meant to preserve. Of course, while such arguments appear persuasive when applied to large contributions to the candidates of major parties, they have less weight when applied to the average $15 contribution to a major-party candidate (which can no longer remain anonymous) or to contributions to minor parties which are not likely to win the election. Finally, defenders argue that disclosure of even relatively small contributions is necessary to insure that substantial contributions in excess of the ceiling are not disguised by breaking them down into smaller payments.

The Supreme Court sustained the broad disclosure rules on their face, while permitting persons who would actually risk some form of retribution or obloquy to secure a judicial exemption from disclosure.

Third, opponents of the Act charge that the public financing of presidential elections discriminates in favor of the Republican and Democratic parties and unfairly freezes minority parties out of the political picture. Defenders of the Act answer that some cutoff is necessary to avoid public funding of nonserious candidacies and that the 5 percent test used by the Act is as fair a cutoff as can be devised. Minor parties argue that it is unrealistic to assume that they can ever achieve the 5 percent figure without preelection subsidy and that providing for postelection payments if the 5 percent test is met is nothing more than a Catch-22 gimmick.

The Supreme Court upheld the public subsidy regulations, arguing that unless "new" parties could raise private funds, they should not qualify for a public subsidy designed to supplant, not substitute for, private financial support.

Finally, opponents of the Act argue that its impact, taken as a whole, is to freeze the political status quo in America. They argue that the tendency of expenditure and contribution ceilings to favor incumbents, coupled with the difficulty which the disclosure provisions and contribution ceiling poses for minority-party fund raising and the overtly discriminatory refusal to permit minority parties to receive preelection subsidies threatens to destroy the viability of our alternative political parties, thus leaving the field to the incumbents of the major parties.

Defenders of the Act respond by minimizing its impact upon minority parties which, they argue, depend primarily upon precisely the type of volunteer labor which has been exempted from the Act's coverage. Moreover, supporters assert, most donations to minority parties fall below the $100 public disclosure limit, and the provision permiting independent expenditures relative to a particular candidate permit a minority party adherent to expend an additional $100 anonymously. Minority-party members respond by pointing out that major parties, in return for giving up the ability to receive large private contributions anonymously, receive an enormous public subsidy, while minority parties, saddled with the same limits on private fund raising (made even more onerous for controversial minority parties by the public-disclosure rules), receive no similar *quid pro quo* of public subsidy, but instead are placed at an even greater competitive disadvantage.

The Supreme Court, by removing restraints on independent and candidate expenditures, ameliorated a portion of the Act's pro-incumbent bias. However, the net position of minority parties in the new electoral order is hardly promising. Minority parties are effectively denied public subsidies while they continue to be subject to contribution limits and disclosure requirements—although a genuinely disfavored minority party should now qualify for an exemption from forced disclosures.

Critics of the 1974 Act argue that every legitimate purpose of the Act could be achieved by a strong, well-enforced law requiring disclosure of contributions in excess of $5,000 to major-party candidates. Supporters of the law scoff at such assertions and point out that only an interrelated set of expenditure and contribution ceilings, coupled with a broad disclosure law and public subsidies, can provide a genuine solution to the problem.

How may an individual give the maximum permissible under the Act as modeled by Buckley v. Valeo?

An individual wishing to maximize his or her contribution to a favored candidate may:

(1) Donate an unlimited amount of time and energy as a volunteer without affecting his or her contribution ceiling or the candidate's expenditure ceiling.

(2) Donate $1,000 directly to the candidate or a political committee supporting him for each primary and general election; and

(3) Expend an unlimited sum in support of the candidate, but not under his direction or control.

Any individual wishing to maximize the total amounts contributed to all candidates may contribute an aggregate of $25,000 in any calendar year to candidates for Federal office. Independent expenditures relative to a candidate are not counted toward the $25,000 maximum. Thus, such an individual may personally expend an unlimited amount of money on Federal campaigns.

An individual wishing to avoid all ceilings on contributions or expenditures may confine himself to commenting on the public issues of the campaign, so long as he does not advocate the defeat or election of a specified candidate. For example, the circulation of material discussing public issues and listing various candidates' positions with respect to those issues would not fall within the Act.

What reports must such an individual file with the Federal Election Committee?

No reports need be filed in connection with the rendition of volunteer sources. Nor need a report be filed in connection with contributions made to a candidate or to a political committee under the candidate's direction and control. It is the responsibility of the candidate to file the appropriate disclosures concerning such a contribution. A report must be filed with the commission, however, in connection with the individual's independent expenditure relative to his favored candidate if it exceeds $100. No report need be filed in connection with expenditures made in connection with a discussion of public issues which does not call for the election or defeat of a clearly identified candidate.

How may an individual retain anonymity in connection with his contributions?

Absolute anonymity may be maintained only for contributions of less than $10. If an individual is prepared to pump $10 bills into a campaign anonymously, apparently no vehicle exists to prevent him from circumventing the Act. However, to the extent that aggregate cash contributions exceed $100, the Act would be violated. Moreover, the number of $10 bills which would have to be pumped before a danger of undue influence exists would be enormous.

Relative anonymity may be maintained for contributions between $10 and $100. Such contributions cause the identity of the contributor to be noted and turned over to the Federal Election Commission, but not made public.

No anonymity may be maintained for contributions or expenditures in excess of $100. They cause the identity of the donor to be publicly disclosed by the candidate at periodic intervals before and after the election.

To the extent that an individual independently expends more than $100 relative to a clearly identified candidate, urging his election or defeat, such individual must file a report with the commission and undergo full public disclosure of his activities. Thus, the purchase of a mimeograph machine and the production and distribution of leaflets supporting a favored candidate must be reported and made public knowledge if more than $100 is expended. If, however, the expenditure is merely to discuss campaign issues without urging the election or defeat of a particular candidate, no reports need be filed no matter how large the expenditure.

What other controls has Congress imposed on the electoral process?

In addition to imposing regulations on campaign financing, Congress has imposed two other broad regulations on the election process. First, it has forbidden most Federal employees to engage in a broad range of partisan political activity; [31] and second, it has outlawed certain political literature.[32] Finally, several state legislatures have sought to impose controls on the content of campaign literature by outlawing false and misleading statements.

Are there restrictions on the political activities of employees of the Federal government?

Yes. Since 1939 the Hatch Act has imposed substantial restrictions on the involvement of Federal civil-service employees (exclusive of presidential appointees) in partisan political activities. By removing the Federal bureaucracy from partisan politics, the Hatch Act is designed to promote government efficiency and neutrality, instill public confidence in the fairness of government, and prevent unscrupulous incumbents from using the vast Federal work force as a partisan election army. It is also designed to insulate Federal employees from pressures from their politically appointed superiors to advance the election prospects of the party in power. Critics of the law, while applauding its purposes, have urged that Federal employees be permitted more latitude to participate in the political life of the country, at least at the local level. The Hatch Act's primary prohibition states that a covered Federal employee "may not take an active part in political management or in political campaigns." In 1970 the United States Civil Service Commission promulgated regulations interpreting the Hatch Act which constitute the current guide to political activity by Federal employees.[33] If an employee is uncertain whether proposed activity would violate the Act, the Civil Service Commission will issue an advisory opinion. An enormous body of obtuse and often contradictory Civil Service Commission rulings exist which attempt to administer the Act. The facial constitutionality of the Hatch Act was sustained by the Supreme Court in 1973.[34]

May a Federal employee engage in any political activity at all?

Certainly. The Hatch Act proscribes only active partisan activity. Thus, Federal employees are free to vote, express individual opinions on the merits of candidates and issues, join a political party and participate in its internal affairs, contribute to the candidate or party of their choice, wear campaign buttons or display bumper stickers, sign nominating petitions, and serve as nonpartisan election officials—such as election judges or registrars. Moreover, the prohibition of the Hatch Act applies only to "partisan" activity. Thus, a Federal employee is free to run as an independent for any office—or to actively support or manage the campaign of any independent candidate. Finally, the Hatch Act has no application to elections involving general public issues such as referenda or bond-approval elections. Thus, a Federal employee may participate without restriction in the campaigns surrounding such elections.

What does the Hatch Act prohibit?

The prohibition on active participation in "political management or in political campaigns" bars a Federal employee from seeking nomination as, or running for election as, the candidate of a partisan political party; serving as the campaign manager of a partisan candidate; serving as a delegate to a party convention; holding internal party office; serving as a poll-watcher for a partisan candidate; organizing a political party or a political club (but not belonging to one already in existence); actively soliciting votes for partisan candidates; initiating or circulating nominating petitions for a partisan candidate; endorsing a partisan candidate in any political advertisement; political broadcast or political literature; and addressing any convention, caucus, rally, or party gathering on behalf of a partisan candidate.

It is often difficult to determine whether given political activity falls on the permitted or proscribed side of the line. The prohibition on active solicitation of votes is difficult to reconcile with the existence of the right of a Federal employee to express his or her individual preference. Moreover, the prohibition on endorsing a partisan candidate in any political advertisement, broadcast, or literature, if read literally, would bar a Federal employee from writing a letter to his newspaper urging the election of a candidate. Finally, the prohibition on addressing a party gathering on behalf of a partisan candidate is difficult to reconcile with an employee's right to join a political party and to participate in its internal affairs. The vagueness and ambiguity of the Hatch Act appears to be among its most serious faults. The willingness of the Civil Service Commission to issue prospective advisory opinions is of some help. However the expense and delay inherent in such a procedure is hardly conducive to active political participation. Violation of the Hatch Act is punishable by dismissal.

Does the Hatch Act cover all government employees?
No. It applies only to Federal employees subject to Civil Service regulation. It has no application to state employees or to presidential appointees exempt from Civil Service control. However, most states have enacted little Hatch Acts which impose similar restrictions on state employees. Although the wording and emphasis of the Little Hatch Acts vary widely from state to state, the administration of the state acts tends to conform to the Federal model. One should assume that a state act is as least as restrictive as the Federal counterpart. Occasionally, state acts are substantially more restrictive. For example, Oklahoma's Act provides that "no employee may . . . ." take part in the management or affairs of any political party or in any political campaign, except to exercise his right as a citizen privately to express his opinion and to cast his

vote." The facial constitutionality of the Oklahoma Act was upheld by the Supreme Court in 1973, with a caveat that in the future, specific applications might violate the First Amendment.[35] Local Hatch Acts have been widely applied to bar police, firemen, teachers, and sanitationmen from engaging in partisan politics. Prior to 1973, a growing body of law had invalidated such restrictions.[36] However, given the Supreme Court's approval of the Hatch Act and its failure to invalidate the Oklahoma version, such restrictions appear valid. They have been recently applied to uphold the suspension of a police officer for sending a letter to his subordinate urging the support of a particular candidate and to ban teachers and assistant district attorneys from running for local office.[37]

May government employees be dismissed for failing to support or contribute to a political party?

In return for giving up the right to engage in partisan politics, government employees not directly engaged in policy setting tasks should be insulated from the wholesale ravages of party patronage. Accordingly, they may not be dismissed because they do not support the party in power. Although earlier cases tolerated the dismissal of ministerial government employees and their replacement by party stalwarts as a holdover of the Jacksonian spoils system, more recent cases condemn the practice as an unconstitutional infringement on belief and free association.[38]

May persons circulate anonymous campaign literature?

Congress and many of the states have provided that campaign literature must reveal the identities of its sponsors and the candidate on whose behalf it is being circulated.[39] The identification requirements are designed to prevent two "dirty tricks" which surfaced during the 1972 campaign. In several legislative races, literature was circulated by the campaign staff of Richard Nixon which appeared to be sponsored by the Democratic candidate and which falsely characterized the Democrat's position in a manner likely to offend many voters. In addition, literature bearing a misleading sponsorship was distributed in several swing legislative districts by Speaker Perry Duryea of the New York State Assembly, urging voters to support a third party in the hope that votes would be drained from one of the major parties.[40] A vigorously enforced requirement of disclosure would prevent such "dirty tricks." Unfortunately, most statutes ban not only literature bearing a false and misleading sponsorship, but anonymous literature as well. Anonymous political literature has played a significant role in the nation's political life and has traditionally received strong constitutional protection.[41] Accordingly, several courts faced with broad antianonymity statutes have invalidated them as unconstitutionally overbroad, while recognizing that a narrow prohibition aimed at false and misleading attribution would be constitutional.

Has any attempt been made to control the content of campaign literature?

Yes. The reformist zeal which fueled the adoption of broad controls on campaign financing inevitably turned to seeking to regulate the content of campaign literature by outlawing malicious, scurrilous, false, or misleading campaign statements. Of course, what appears "false and misleading" to one candidate is deemed ultimate truth by another. Whether such attempts to determine "truth" in campaigning can survive First Amendment scrutiny is doubtful. New York's experiment has already been invalidated.[42]

May campaigning be prohibited on election day?

No. While the traditional requirement that campaigning be curtailed in the actual polling place is undoubtedly valid, attempts to forbid electioneering on election day have universally been invalidated.

Do candidates have a right of access to the media?

Candidates have no right to access to the press, either to purchase advertisements or to gain equal coverage. The Supreme Court has ruled that the First Amendment prohibits the enforcement of a right of access to the press.[43]

Although the broadcast media are, of course, protected by the First Amendment, candidates do have limited access rights to radio and television. While candidates, under current law, do not possess a "right" to purchase commercial air time,[44] if a broadcaster makes commercial air time available to one candidate, it must make time available under the same rates to his opponents. Moreover, if one candidate secures substantial blocs of air time, either commercially or because of an imbalance in news coverage, the broadcaster may be required, under the "fairness doctrine," [45] to make free air time available to *bona fide* opponents. Finally, if free campaign time is given to any candidate, compensatory "equal time" must be made available to opponents.

NOTES

1. Buckley v. Valeo, 96 S. Ct. 32 (1976).
2. The history of our attempt to regulate campaign financing prior to the F.E.C.A. is related in the Circuit

Court's opinion in Buckley v. Valeo, at 519 F.2d 821 (D.C.Cir. 1975).

3. The 1974 version of the F.E.C.A. is set out at Pub. L. No. 92–225, 86 Stat. 3, as amended, Pub. L. 93–443, 83 Stat. 1263.

4. The Act defines a "contribution" at 18 U.S.C. §591(e) (1) and (2).

5. §591(e) (5) (A)-(D).

6. 18 U.S.C. §591 (b).

7. United States v. National Committee for Impeachment, 469 F.2d 1131 (2d Cir. 1972); ACLU v. Jennings, 366 F. Supp. 1041 (D.D.C. 1973) vacated as moot sub. nom. Staats v. ACLU, 422 U.S. 1030 (1975).

8. 18 U.S.C. §591(d).

9. 18 U.S.C. §610.

10. Schwartz v. Romnes, 495 F.2d 844 (2d Cir. 1974).

11. Cort. v. Ash, 95 S. Ct. 2080 (1975).

12. 18 U.S.C. §§611, 613.

13. 18 U.S.C. §608.

14. 18 U.S.C. §608(c).

15. 18 U.S.C. §608(c) (1) (C), (D).

16. 18 U.S.C. §608(c) (1) (C)-(E).

17. 18 U.S.C. §608(c) (1) (A), (B).

18. 18 U.S.C. §608(d).

19. The Act's disclosure provisions are set at 2 U.S.C. §431 et. seq.

20. 2 U.S.C. §434(e).

21. Provisions governing public financing of presidential campaigns are now set forth at Title 26 U.S.C. §§6096 and Subchapter H, §§9001-9042.

22. 26 U.S.C. §9002(6), (7) and (8).

23. 26 U.S.C. §9008(d).

24. 26 U.S.C. §9004(a)(1).

25. 26 U.S.C. §§ 9003 (b).

26. 26 U.S.C. §9004(a) (3). An additional requirement for minor and new parties is that they appear on the ballot in at least 10 states. §9002 (2) (B).

27. 26 U.S.C. §§9033-9037.

28. 26 U.S.C. §§§9033(b) (3), (4).

29. 26 U.S.C. §9034(a).

30. 2 U.S.C. 438 et. seq.

31. 5 U.S.C. §7324(a) (2).
32. 18 U.S.C. §612.
33. 5 C.F.R. pt. 733.
34. United States Civil Service Comm. v. Nat'l. Ass'n of Letter Carriers, 413 U.S. 548 (1973).
35. Broadrick v. Oklahoma, 413 U.S. 601 (1973).
36. E.g. Mancuso v. Taft, 476 F.2d 187 (1st Cir. 1973).
37. Paulos v. Breier, 371 F. Supp. 523 (E.D. Wis. 1974) aff'd, 507 F.2d 1383 (7th Cir. 1974).
38. E.g. Nunnery v. Barber, 503 F.2d 1349 (4th Cir. 1974); Burns v. Elrod, 509 F.2d 1133 (7th Cir. 1975).
39. 18 U.S.C §612.
40. People v. Duryea, 351 NYS2d 978, aff'd 354 NYS2d 129 (1974).
41. E.g. Talley v. California, 362 U.S. 60 (1960).
42. Vanasco v. Schwartz, 401 F. Supp. 87 (EDNY 1975) aff'd 96 S. Ct. 763 (1976).
43. Miami Herald Publishing Co. v. Tornillo, 418 U.S. 241 (1974).
44. Columbia Broadcasting System v. Democratic National Committee, 412 U.S. 94 (1973).
45. Red Lion Broadcasting Co. v. Federal Communications Comm'n, 395 U.S. 367 (1969).

VIII

The Constitutional Status of Political Parties

The Federal Constitution contains no discussion regarding the role or function of political parties within the American system of government. The omission by those who drafted the document was neither unconscious nor inadvertent; but rather reflective of the widespread hostility toward political parties that characterized eigtheenth-century political philosophy. "Party," wrote Jonathan Swift, "is the madness of many, for the gain of the few." [1] And America's Founding Fathers, however disparate their views on other matters, united in their agreement with Swift's condemnation of parties—or "factions" as they were opprobriously called. Thus, Madison in the *Federalist Paper* No. 10, inveighed against the "violence of faction." [2] Hamilton was even more vigorous in his opposition to parties, as he urged the ratification of the Federal Constitution as a means "to abolish factions and to unite all parties for the general welfare." [3] John Adams was similarly unstinting in his criticism of political parties. He argued that they "destroyed all sense and understanding, all equity and humanity, all memory and regard to truth, all virtue, honor, decorum and veracity." [4] And Washington, in his farewell address, warned "against the baneful effects of the Spirit of Party generally." [5]

Despite nearly unanimous concern by the framers of the Constitution regarding the destructive potential of partisanship, the Federal Constitution was barely ratified and the government just starting to function when organized factions began to emerge. It is ironic, and perhaps indicative of political expediency, that the leading opponents of factionalism soon became the primary architects of a coordinated party system.

But the rift between the Federalists and the Jeffersonian Republicans which structured the rise of partisan opposition in the United States is well known and needs no rehearsal here.[6] What is curious and deserving of some explanation is why sophisticated politicians, as were the Founding Fathers, should have completely failed to anticipate the development of a party system. A partial explanation, suggested by Richard Hofstadter, is that,

"[t]he idea of a legitimate opposition—recognized opposition, organized and free enough in its activities to be able to displace an existing government by peaceful means—[was] an immensely sophisticated idea, and it was not an idea that the Fathers found fully developed and ready to hand when they began their enterprise in republican constitutionalism in 1788." [7]

Yet another partial answer may be that the practical emergence of partisan opposition within a democratic society was not entirely unanticipated—even by those who were ideally opposed to its development. Madison, for example, recognized that "the latent causes of faction are . . . sown in the nature of man." [8] Unless one were willing to suppress all political dissent and opposition, the development of partisanship was probably an inevitable consequence of a free society. Indeed, the inevitable development of organized partisanship as a natural concomitant of an increasingly democratized society has been brilliantly demonstrated by V. O. Key, who observed that:

> "As democratic ideas corroded the old foundations of authority, members of the old governing elite reached out to legitimize their positions under the new notions by appealing for popular support. That appeal compelled deference to popular views, but it also required the development of organization to communicate with and to manage the electorate. Thus, members of a parliamentary body, who earlier occupied their seats as an incident to the ownership of property or as a perquisite of class position, had to defer to the people—or to those who had the suffrage—and to create electoral organizations to rally voters to their support. In a sense, government, left suspended in mid-air by the erosion of the old justifications for its authority, had to build new foundations in the new environment of a democratic ideology." [9]

V. O. Key's phenomenological analysis of the development of political parties in democratic societies is suggestive of the forces that, in large measure, impelled the cultivation of a party system in the United States. It does not, however, explain why the United States developed a two-party system rather than a multiparty system. And it does not explain why the two major parties in that system tend to be non-ideological. Several theories have been advanced in an attempt to explain America's non-ideological two-party system. Maurice Duverger, for example, offers the suggestion that the two-party system is merely a natural product of the inherent duality in politics. Duverger claims that "the two-party system seems to correspond to the nature of things, that is to say that political choice usually takes the form of a choice between two alternatives. A duality of parties does not always exist, but almost always there is a duality of tendencies." [10] Some commentators have been more hard-edged in their suggestions that two-party politics is the product of certain structural features within America's Federal system. The structuralists contend, for example, that "the practice of choosing representatives from single-member districts by a plurality vote in contrast with systems of proportional representation which are based on multimember districts," [11] effectively eliminates third parties. In a single-member district, it is argued, "only two parties can contend for electoral victory with any hope of success; a third party is doomed to perpetual defeat unless it can manage to absorb the following of one of the major parties and thereby become one of them." [12] Structuralists also suggest that the popular election of the President results in two-party politics because under such a practice there can be only one national winner. Therefore, the "Presidency, unlike a multiparty cabinet, cannot be parceled out among miniscule parties. . . . [And] [t]he necessity of uniting to have a chance of sharing in a victory in a [national] presidential campaign pulls the state party organizations together." [13] Others argue that the selection of the Chief Executive, not by the dominant congressional party but by a separate popular election, results in the non-ideological nature of the two major parties. It is observed that in the typical European parliamentarian system, coalitions are struck after the popular election in order to select a head of state from among the dominant legislative coalition. But the independent national election of a president causes the contenders to form their coalitions in advance of the election. And the coalitions thus concluded tend to encompass a wide range of diverse ideologies. The political parties that form these coalitions, therefore, tend to be non-ideological.

Other students of the political process offer different explanations for the non-ideological nature of America's two-party system. Dennis Brogan attempts to explain why politics in America differs so significantly from the typical European democracies, where the parties tend to divide along lines of economic philosophy. Brogan concludes that much of the explanation pertains to the vastly pluralistic nature of American society. Quoting from Dewey Anderson and Percy E. Davidson, Brogan suggests that in the United States "[p]olitical interests are not economic alone. Matters of taste, habit, culture and morals cut across economic group lines at times to suggest strong affinities between voters in widely separated economic groups." [14]

Brogan, however, also offers a variety of other explanations—some analytical and some visceral—for the perpetuation of a two-party system in the United States. He suggests organizational and temporal impediments that dissuade the development of third parties. He notes: "The linking up of national and state, and often municipal elections, forces some degree of common action at all levels. It requires a great deal of tenacity to hold on while a party slowly builds up enough support to win the offices that make it more than a mere body of organized protest. Most voters do not have the tenacity; most politicians do not have it either." [15] Brogan also allows that the two-party system is reinforced by a variety of election laws, such as those regarding access to the ballot, that are intentionally designed to discriminate against third parties. "Neither party has an interest in making things easy for a third party," chides Brogan, "and neither party tries to make it easy." [16] It is probably the case, however, that no single explanation of the development and perpetuation of America's two-party system is sufficient. As Professor Key has concluded "[t]he safest explanation is that several factors conspired toward the development of the American dual party pattern. These included the accidents of history that produced dual divisions on great issues at critical points in our history, the consequences of our institutional forms, the clustering of popular opinions around a point of central consensus rather than their bipolarization, and perhaps others. The assignment of weights to each of these is an enterprise too uncertain to be hazarded." [17]

The most formidable criticism of America's two-party structure is that such a system breeds "consensus" politics in which neither major political party possesses a distinctive ideological commitment. As Clinton Rossiter has shown, the major parties "are creatures of compromise, coalitions of interest in which principle is muted and even silenced." [18] Many persons seriously question whether contemporary American society can afford the luxury of a political system in which "principle is muted and even silenced" and in which the major parties lack serious ideological commitment.

Yet, in spite of this very serious criticism of the two-party system, America's development of that system continues to represent among its most significant contributions to the practice of democratic government. For by institutionalizing dissent into organized party conflict, political opposition became legitimized —and peaceful. As Professor Key has pointed out, "Party operations provided a substitute for revolt and insurrection and a new means for determining succession to authority. As the party process took form the workability of organized non-violent conflict for control of government became established." [19]

But, political parties in their modern institutionalized form have come to suffer from a kind of schizophrenic personality derivative of their dual organizational functions and their ambivalent constitutional status. The parties are in many respects voluntary political associations and therefore protected by the First Amendment from governmental encroachment upon their associational freedoms. But in other respects political parties "have become so inextricably intertwined in the States' election process" as to represent "an integral and critical phase of [that] overall process." [20] In such a circumstance, the political parties are surrogate governmental agencies and as such become subject to the restraints imposed upon governmental institutions by the Federal Constitution. The earliest and still perhaps most striking example of the imposition of constitutional limitations upon political parties occurred in the so-called *White Primary* cases involving the State of Texas.[21] Texas had, through a variety of devices, delegated to the political parties within the state the authority to establish qualifications for voting in the state's primary elections. The political parties had consistently employed this delegated authority to exclude blacks from voting in the primaries. Accordingly, in a series of cases the Supreme Court found it necessary to impose constitutional sanctions upon the political parties to the extent that they were engaging in racially discriminatory practices.[22] Thus political parties as surrogate governmental institutions often find themselves at odds and in conflict with the rights of certain voters and candidates. On other occasions political parties as private and voluntary agglomerations of voters and candidates often find themselves at odds and in conflict with the demands of government. Following is a discussion of these kinds of conflicts. But in determining the rights of voters and candidates vis-à-vis the political parties and the rights of parties vis-à-vis the government, the threshold inquiry must always implicitly involve an examination as to whether, under the facts of the particular dispute, the political party is acting as a voluntary private association or as a surrogate governmental agency. Only when the party acts as a governmental agency is it subject to constitutional restraints.

How do political parties select candidates?

The two principal methods by which political parties select candidates are through primary elections, or, alternatively, by means of party conventions. The particular method employed for selecting candidates is usually dictated by state law, which typically prescribes different methods for candidate selection depending upon whether the political party is deemed a major or minor party. Accordingly, as a general proposition, parties that possess sufficient popular support to be regarded as major parties, and thereby qualify for automatic ballot status, are most often required to select their candidates by means of primary elections. Smaller parties, parties that do not qualify for automatic ballot status, or parties that would be attempting to qualify for ballot status for the first time, are often required to choose their candidates at conventions or caucuses.[23]

Different rules and procedures, however, pertain to the selection of presidential and vice-presidential candidates. Candidates for these offices are chosen at national nominating conventions which are attended by delegates from each state. State laws regarding the selection of delegates to the national convention fall, generally, into three categories. In about eighteen states and in the District of Columbia, delegates to the national presidential conventions are chosen in primary elections. In twenty states, parties possess the option of choosing their delegates by means of primary elections or conventions. And in twelve states the delegates must be chosen by either convention or caucus procedures.[24]

Can potential voters be excluded by state law from the party's candidate selection process?

Yes. In an attempt to protect the cohesiveness and stability of political parties, many states have enacted laws that regulate the circumstances under which individuals may participate in a party's candidate selection process or otherwise affiliate with a party.

Do such laws which seek to protect party cohesiveness require that potential affiliates with the party declare their allegiance to the party?

Yes, quite frequently. It is probably the case that the cohesive attributes of the two major parties are power and patronage rather than ideology and principle. Indeed, it is commonly observed that the American political arrangement, involving as it does, a federal system of government, two major political parties, and a president selected not by the dominant congressional party but independently elected by popular vote, results in the practice of "consensus" politics in which neither of the two major parties possesses a distinctive, distinguishable or consistent ideology. Nevertheless, each political party perceives itself as possessing a particular ideology which is worthy of statutory protection. Accordingly, a majority of state legislatures have enacted laws that are protective of the parties' perceived interests. Such election laws, seeking to protect party cohesion, continue to focus upon the concept of a common political ideology within each party. These laws in their broadest reach are constructed to insure that persons participating in the affairs, and particularly in the nominating process of a party, share similar political and ideological beliefs. The enactments unite in the requirement that persons seeking to affiliate with a party and vote in the party's primary election must declare their affinity for the principles and values of the party. In some instances the declarant must also pledge to support those candidates who will be ultimately nominated by the parties, although such pledges are clearly unenforceable.

The major variations from state to state in such laws requiring declarations of affinity turn upon the point in time when such declarations must be made. Some states allow the declarations to be made immediately before the party's primary election and occasionally even on the day of the election. Other states require, as a condition precedent to voting in the primary, that the voter enroll and declare affiliation with the party substantially in advance of the election. Such laws which require declarations of affiliation well in advance of the elections are called "durational affiliation" provisions.

These "durational affiliation" requirements are designed to address more specific and realistic concerns than the largely illusory interest in ideological affinity among party members. These requirements are intended to prevent electoral practices such as "interparty raiding" from destroying the stability and cohesiveness of parties.

"Inter-party Raiding" is an organized scheme whereby voters affiliated with one party attempt to vote in a rival party's primary election in order to elect a weak candidate from the rival party so that the rival will be more easily defeated by the genuinely preferred party at the general election. But, in addition to the problem of voters crossing party lines for the purposes of raiding, many state laws, either inadvertently or by design, effectively limit other less malevolent sorts of cross-over voting. For example, certain voters of one party affiliation may seek to vote in the rival party's primary election, not for the purpose of nominating a weak candidate in the rival party, but for the purpose of nominating a palatable second choice from the rival party. Such a practice insures that if the candidate from the voter's genuine party loses, the candidate from the rival party will be an acceptable second choice. Yet another variety of cross-over voting involves the voter, who although affiliated with one party, actually prefers the candidate in another party over all other candidates regardless of party. In such a circumstance the voter may wish to cross over for that particular election and genuinely support the candidate in the rival party. Because it is difficult to accurately determine or even to inquire into the motives of persons seeking to vote in rival parties' primary elections, the typical durational affiliation laws have been broadly drafted to limit all cross-over voting.

But, in part, because of their breadth, the "durational affiliation" requirements have been the subject of recent litigation upon the theory that such laws unnecessarily and indiscriminately abridge the rights of certain persons to vote in primary elections. For example, Illinois had enacted a law that prohibited a person from voting in a political party's primary election if such person had voted in another party's primary within the preceding twenty-three months. The Illinois law was challenged by Harriet Pontikes who as "a qualified Chicago voter . . . had voted in a Republican primary in February 1971; [who] wanted to vote in a March 1972 Democratic primary; but was barred from doing so by [the] 23-month rule." [25] The state defended the rule on the grounds that it was necessary to prevent "raiding." The Supreme Court, however, rejected this defense. The Court observed that the "freedom to associate with others for the common advancement of political beliefs and ideas is a form of 'orderly group activity' protected by the First and Fourteenth Amendments." [26] The Court further found that the Illinois law had the effect "of 'locking' a voter into an unwanted party affiliation from one election to the next. . . . and the only way to break the 'lock' is to forego voting in *any* primary for a period of almost two years." [27] The Court, therefore, concluded that the Illinois "durational affiliation" requirement unconstitutionally abridged the "right of free political association protected by the First and Fourteenth Amendments." [28]

It must be noted, however, that the Supreme Court had reached a different conclusion during the preceding judicial term, when it reviewed New York's durational affiliation scheme and upheld its validity. New York had required that persons must enroll with a party during the voter registration period that preceded the general election in order to vote in a subsequent party primary election. Consequently, the New York law had the effect of excluding some persons from voting in party primary elections unless such persons had enrolled with a party more than eleven months before the election in which such persons wished to vote. As in the *Pontikes* case, persons who were deprived of the right to vote by the New York "durational affiliation" requirement challenged the source of that deprivation. As in *Pontikes,* such persons argued that the New York statutory scheme abridged their constitutional right of associational freedom and, concomitantly, their right to affiliate with the party of their choice. As in *Pontikes*, the state defended the law on the grounds that the requirements were necessary to prevent "raiding." But unlike the *Pontikes* case, in the

New York situation the Supreme Court upheld the constitutionality of the pertinent durational affiliation provisions.[29]

This discrepancy in result, between the adjudication of the New York durational affiliation scheme and the Illinois provision, is not easily explicable. In many respects the New York law which was upheld is far more restrictive of the franchise than the Illinois enactment which was invalidated. The Illinois law was limited only to persons who wanted to change affiliation from one party to another. The New York law, however, applied to all persons seeking to vote in a party's primary regardless of prior affiliation. Accordingly, for the person not previously affiliated with a party and for persons who did not participate in the preceding primary election the Illinois "durational affiliation" law is inapplicable. But, the New York provision would bar many of these individuals from voting. The Illinois law is more restrictive than that of New York only in the narrow circumstance of the previously affiliated voter, who has voted with one party in a previous primary election and who wishes to vote in another party's primary at a subsequent election. But, the circumstance—involving the previously affiliated voter—to which the Illinois law is specifically addressed, is, as a practical matter, the only situation in which the danger of raiding is even a remote possibility. Thus, if the prevention of "raiding" represents the underlying rationale for these durational affiliation laws, the Illinois approach appears more direct and more carefully tailored to the problem of "raiding" than the New York law.

The Supreme Court attempted to distinguish the New York law from the Illinois provision by suggesting that [u]nder the New York law a person who wanted to vote in a different party primary every year was not precluded from doing so; he had only to meet the requirement of declaring his party allegiance 30 days before the preceding general election." [30] But, in fact, the real difference in result seems to derive from the fact that the persons challenging the New York provision could have voted in the New York primary election if they had attempted to enroll earlier, whereas Ms. Pontikes was absolutely foreclosed from voting in the 1972 Democratic primary by the Illinois enactment.

Do affiliation laws impose limitations upon persons seeking to become party nominees?

Yes. Affiliation laws that limit potential voter participation in primary elections similarly limit potential candidate access to the election ballot. A majority of states require that persons seeking to secure a nomination from a party as a candidate or as a delegate must declare their affinity for the principles and values of the party. Moreover, a significant number of states impose "durational affiliation" requirements, such as those previously discussed, upon persons seeking party nominations.[31]

The same justifications that are advanced in support of the imposition of durational affiliation laws for voters are used to justify similar provisions for candidates. With regard to prospective candidates as with potential voters, affiliation laws are said to protect the stability of political parties by preventing the practice of "raiding." The practice of raiding by candidates, however, differs from voter raiding schemes insofar as candidate raiding requires significantly less conspiratorial organization. The technique of raiding by candidates has been described in the following manner:

". . . [M]embers of one party will run in the primary of an opposing party either to divert votes from a strong candidate, thereby securing the nomination of a weak candidate, or to win the nomination of the opposing party and then deliberately run a lackluster campaign against the nominee of the candidate's real party."[32]

As discussed earlier, in order to be effective, raiding by voters requires organized and elaborate complicity among many persons. But, as just seen, raiding by a duplicitous candidate can be effective even if undertaken by a single individual acting alone. For this reason, it is claimed that "durational affiliation" laws for candidates are more vital for the protection of parties than similar provisions pertaining to voters. And the courts have reacted to such claims by generally upholding such provisions. Indeed, the Supreme Court has, in *Lippitt* v. *Cipollone*,[33] summarily affirmed a lower court ruling upholding a four-year durational affiliation requirement for candidates. But several remarks of caution must accompany the suggestion that a four-year durational affiliation provision for candidates violates no constitutional strictures. First, it must be observed that the validation of the four-year provision in the *Lippitt* case was affirmed by the Supreme Court by a narrow 5–4 vote. Second, it should be remembered that the Supreme Court did not reach its decision in the *Lippitt* case after a full briefing of the issues and after a plenary argument. Rather, the court disposed of the case pursuant to its practice of treating some cases in a summary manner. Accordingly, the Court wrote no opinion in the case. Finally, it should be noted that the Supreme Court decision in the *Lippitt* case preceded the Court's invalidation of the Illinois 23-month durational affiliation law for voters in the *Pontikes* case. Therefore, in light of the subsequent decision in the *Pontikes* case, the continued viability of the *Lippitt* decision may be seriously questioned. It therefore remains unclear whether a four-year durational affiliation law for candidates would survive contemporary constitutional scrutiny.

New York has adopted an interesting and somewhat flexible approach to the problem of raiding by candidates. New York does impose, as a general rule, a durational affiliation requirement for persons seeking to run in a party primary. But this general rule is not absolute. New York allows each party the discretion to deviate from the general rule when it wishes, in order to permit a non-affiliate to run in the party's own primary. The New York approach adopts the rationale that, inasmuch as durational affiliation laws are intended for the protection of the parties, it is the parties who should, in each instance, make the ultimate decision as to whether they require the protection that the law would confer. Moreover, the New York approach has the additional virtue of granting to the parties the capacity to facilitate fusion tickets by permitting non-affiliates to run in party primary elections.

Despite these virtues New York's flexible durational affiliation approach regarding candidates is not without its difficulties. It is claimed that in achieving flexibility, New York confers unfettered discretion upon the political parties to grant or deny ballot status to certain citizens. It is further contended that such a standardless delegation of authority violates both the due process and equal protection clauses of the Federal Constitution in instances in which the abuse of the delegated discretion implicates an interest so fundamental as the right to run for office. This was precisely the claim advanced by Ramsey Clark when, in 1974, the Liberal Party refused to allow him to run as a candidate for the United States Senate in the Liberal Party primary election. In the face of Mr. Clark's challenge, however, a Federal court upheld the validity of the New York law upon the finding that New York's interests in facilitating fusion tickets, in preventing voter confusion by limiting the number of candidates, and in protecting parties against raiding were all legitimate purposes within the electoral process.[34]

But raiding is not the only sort of electoral deception at which durational affiliation laws are aimed. In addition to the problem of raiding by candidates, difficulties are presented by persons who fail to secure their regular party nominations and who subsequently attempt to run as independent candidates. It is contended that the independent candidacies of these "sore losers" renders the political process even more factious and less efficient than it presently is. Accordingly, writing for the Supreme Court, Mr. Justice White has argued that,

"[t]he direct primary . . . is not merely an exercise or warm-up for the general election but an integral part of the entire election process, the initial stage in a two-stage process by which the people choose their public officers. It functions to winnow out and finally reject all but the chosen candidates. The . . . general policy is to have contending forces within the party employ the primary campaign and primary election to finally settle their differences. The general election ballot is reserved for major struggles; it is not a forum for continuing intraparty feuds." [35]

In reliance upon this line of argument a number of states have enacted laws to prevent the "sore losers" in party primary elections from subsequently running as independent candidates in the general elections. Some states have enacted specific and direct prohibitions, to the effect that a person who runs in a party primary election cannot subsequently run as an independent candidate in the general election. Other states attempt to achieve the same result by requiring independent candidates to file their applications for ballot status prior to the party primary elections and to further prohibit announced independents from running for party nominations as well. Still other states prohibit persons from qualifying as independent candidates unless such persons had previously renounced their party affiliation well in advance of the general election. These states adopt, in a sense, "durational disaffiliation" provisions. One such state is California, which prohibits "ballot position to an independent candidate for elective public office if he [or she] voted in the immediately preceding primary [citations omitted], or if he [or she] had a registered affiliation with a qualified political party at any time within one year prior to the immediately preceding primary election [citations omitted]." [36] The California law had the effect of requiring persons affiliated with a party to take affirmative steps to disaffiliate up to seventeen months before the general election in order to run as an independent candidate in the general election. To the extent that the California law prohibited independent candidacies not only of persons who ran and lost in the party primary elections but also of persons who were party affiliates even if they in no way participated in a preceding primary election, the California enactment seems unnecessarily broad in its application and difficult to justify. Nevertheless, in a 1974 decision [37] the Supreme Court upheld the constitutionality of these provisions upon the general conclusion that such requirements maintained the stability of the political process. How or why such laws maintained the stability of the political process was not fully explained. Nevertheless, in light of the 1974 decision "durational disaffiliation" laws, such as that in California, which bar independent candidacies are apparently valid.

When party rulemaking conflicts with state or even national law, will the party ruling be required to yield?

Not necessarily. As noted earlier, political parties are in many respects voluntary political associations and, accordingly, protected by the First Amendment from governmental abridgement of their associational freedoms. In other instances, however, political parties are so "inextricably intertwined" in the electoral process as to be regarded as surrogate governmental agencies. Thus party rules that pertain to the nomination of candidates, or the administering of special elections, or the granting of consent to non-affiliates who wish to run in primary elections, are so intimately connected with the electoral process as to render such party functions subject to governmental limitations. On the other hand, when the party engages in activity pertaining to its own internal management or to the establishment of party platforms and strategies, it is engaging in the sort of private associational activity that is protected by the First Amendment from governmental control. Thus, when there is a conflict between a state law and a party rule or decision, as a general rule, the resolution of that conflict will depend upon whether the party ruling is inextricably implicated within the electoral process or whether the ruling pertains only to a private party matter.

There are special circumstances where the general methodological approach just described is not terribly useful for determining the validity of party rules that conflict with governmental enactments. A variety of such special circumstances are presented by the national presidential nominating conventions. The national presidential convention seems to entail party activity in its most public function when the party nominates the presidential candidate. But the convention also encompasses extensive private associational activity such as the drafting of the party platform and the development of party strategies. Because of this omnibus nature of presidential nominating conventions, conflicts between state laws and party rules pertaining to the conduct of the conventions have been particularly troubling to the courts that have been called upon to adjudicate such matters. Thus, for example, in 1972, there was a conflict between an Illinois state law and the rules of the Democratic Party which resulted in a dispute regarding the seating of certain Illinois delegates at the Democratic national convention. In the case of *Wigoda* v. *Cousins* the issue was brought to the Illinois state courts, which held that "the law of the state is supreme and party rules to the contrary are of no effect." [38] The Supreme Court, however, reversed the decision of the Illinois court.[39] The Supreme Court decision in *Cousins* rested, in large measure, upon the Court's perception of both the omnibus quality to the national presidential conventions and the First Amendment values which protect the party's associational rights of self-regulation. But the Court also noted that "the pervasive national interest" furthered by the quadrennial party conventions "is greater than any interest of an individual state." [40] This latter observation by the Court lends support to the suggestion that the future applicability of the *Cousins* ruling might be limited only to instances where there is a conflict between state laws and national party rules. Accordingly, it is contended by some that in the circumstance of a conflict between a party rule and a Congressional enactment the principles enunciated in the *Cousins* case would not be controlling. Similarly, it is claimed that the principles of the *Cousins* case would be inapposite in the circumstance of a conflict between a state law and local party rules pertaining to a nominating convention for state office. Of course, each of these contentions depends upon a reading of the *Cousins* decision which gives great weight to the Court's conclusion regarding the pervasive quality of national conventions as opposed to purely parochial interests advanced by local state law. And such a reading of the *Cousins* decision is entirely speculative. Consequently, several questions regarding the limits of the *Cousins* case and the parameters of party autonomy remain unclear.

In the context of national conventions, there is one special circumstance in which parties are probably subject to governmental limitations. Where national party rules regarding the selection of delegates do come in conflict with the Federal constitutional requirement of "one person-one vote" the courts and commentators have suggested that, despite the parties' countervailing interest in associational freedom, the delegate selection process must satisfy the principle pertaining to one person-one vote.[41] But, in spite of the one person-one vote line of cases, it cannot be safely concluded that national party ruling must yield whenever it conflicts with constitutional principles. Indeed, conflicts between party rules and Federal constitutional principles present a classic confrontation between countervailing constitutional principles. On the one hand, the party's associational interest in rule making and self-regulation is itself protected by the First Amendment. On the other hand the party may in some instances be exercising its rule-making authority in a manner violative of other constitutional values. That was precisely the problem presented at the 1972 Democratic Convention, when the Credentials Committee of the Democratic Party ruled, on the eve of the convention, that California's winner-take-all primary election was unfair and failed to advance the party's interest in a delegation that proportionately represented the full range of voter sentiment. The decision of the Credentials Committee had the effect of unseating many of Senator McGovern's delegates and replacing them with delegates who were supporters of Senator Humphrey. The unseated McGovern delegates repaired to Federal district court but were denied relief. They appealed to the Court of Appeals for the District of Columbia which reversed the lower court.[42] The Court of Appeals held that the McGovern delegates were denied due process by the decision which unseated them because the rules of the Democratic Party prior to the convention had not prohibited winner-take-all primaries. Thus the decision of the Court of Appeals squarely presented a conflict between two competing constitutional values. The party decision was said to violate the due process clause; yet the party's decision-making capacity was said to be free from any governmental interference by the associational freedom provision of the First Amendment. Accordingly, the constitutional conflict was presented to the Supreme Court which expressed "grave doubts as to the action taken by the Court of Appeals." [43] In discussing its reservations the Court pointed out that judicial intrusion into party disputes "traditionally has been approached with great caution and restraint" [44] and that the convention itself might be a more appropriate "forum for determining intra-party disputes as to which delegates should be seated." [45] The Court observed that the case involved "[h]ighly important questions . . . concerning justiciability, whether the action of the Credentials Committee is state action, and if so the reach of the Due Process Clause . . . [and] [v]ital rights of association. . . ." [46] But the Court ultimately chose not to resolve those questions. Instead the Court elected to reverse the order of the Court of Appeals below but to take no action regarding the application for review. In effect, the Court decided not to decide the case. Consequently, the question of whether the freedom of association protective of party autonomy must, as a general rule, yield to other countervailing constitutional considerations remains unresolved.

NOTES

1. J. Swift, Thoughts on Various Subjects.
2. A. Hamilton, J. Madison, and J. Jay, The Federalist Papers, ed. and intro. by C. Rossiter, (New American Library, 1961). "Federalist Paper No. 10" at p. 77.
3. R. Hofstadter, The Idea of a Party System, (1970) at p. 17.
4. Quoted in Hofstadter, supra, at p. 28.
5. H.S. Commager, ed. Documents in American History (6th ed., 1958), "Washington's Farewell Address" (Sept. 17, 1796) at pp. 169, 172.
6. The development of America's two-party system is presented in R. Hofstadter, The Idea of a Party System (1970); J.M. Burns, The Deadlock of Democracy (1963); and J. Charles, the Origins of the American Party System, (1956).
7. Hofstadter, supra at p. 8.
8. The Federalist Papers, supra at p. 79.
9. V.O. Key, Politics, Parties & Pressure Groups, (5th ed., 1964) at p. 201.
10. M. Duverger, Political Parties (1954), at p. 215.
11. Key, supra at p. 208
12. Ibid.
13. Ibid. at p. 209.
14. D.W. Brogan, Politics in America (Anchor ed., 1954, 1960) at p. 64 quoting from D. Anderson and P.E. Davidson, Ballots and the Democratic Class Struggle (1943) pp. 255-257.
15. Brogan, supra at p. 63.
16. Ibid.
17. Key, supra at p. 210.

18. C. Rossiter, Parties and Politics in America (1960) p. 20.
19. Key, supra at p. 205.
20. Redfearn v. Delaware Republican State Committee 362 F. Supp. 65, 70-71 (D. Del., 1973).
21. Terry v. Adams 345 U.S. 461 (1953); Smith v. Allwright 321 U.S. 649 (1944); Grovey v. Townsend 295 U.S. 45 (1935); Nixon v. Condon 286 U.S. 73 (1932); Nixon v. Herndon 273 U.S. 536 (1927).
22. See Terry v. Adams 345 U.S. 461 (1953).
23. For a compilation of the laws in each state pertaining to political parties' candidate selection process see "Developments in the Law—Elections," 88 Harv. L. Rev. 1111, 1152-1153, fns. 5-11, (1975).
24. For a compilation of the laws in each state pertaining to the selection of delegates to the national presidential nominating conventions see "Developments in the Law—Elections," 88 Harv. L. Rev. 1111, 1153-1154, fns. 12-15 (1975).
25. Kusper v. Pontikes 414 U.S. 51, 52-53 (1973).
26. Kusper v. Pontikes, supra at 56-57.
27. Kusper v. Pontikes, supra at 60-61.
28. Kusper v. Pontikes, supra at 61.
29. Rosario v. Rockefeller 410 U.S. 752 (1973).
30. Kusper v. Pontikes, supra at 60.
31. For a compilation of state laws that impose party affiliation requirements upon potential candidates see "Developments in the Law—Elections," 88 Harv. L. Rev. 1111, 1175-1176 (1975).
32. "Developments in the Law—Elections," 88 Harv. L. Rev. 1111, 1178 (1975).
33. Lippitt v. Cipollone 337 F. Supp. 1405 (N.D. Ohio, 1971), aff'd 404 U.S. 1032 (1972).
34. Clark v. Rose, 379 F. Supp. 73 (S.D.N.Y. 1974).
35. Storer v. Brown, 415 U.S. 724, 735 (1974).
36. Storer v. Brown, supra at 721.
37. Storer v. Brown, 415 U.S. 724 (1974).
38. Wigoda v. Cousins 14 Ill. App. 3d 460, 475, 302 N.E. 2d 614, 627 (1973).
39. Cousins v. Wigoda 419 U.S. 477 (1975).
40. Cousins v. Wigoda, supra at 490.
41. See supra Chapter V.

42. Brown v. O'Brien 469 F.2d 563 (D.C. Cir. 1972).
43. O'Brien v. Brown, 409 U.S. 1, 5 (1972).
44. O'Brien v. Brown, supra at 4.
45. Ibid.
46. Ibid.

DISCUS BOOKS
DISTINGUISHED NON-FICTION

American Civil Liberties Union Handbooks
on The Rights of Americans

THE RIGHTS OF CANDIDATES AND VOTERS
B. Neuborne and A. Eisenberg   28159   1.50

THE RIGHTS OF MENTAL PATIENTS
Bruce Ennis and Loren Siegel   10652   1.25

THE RIGHTS OF THE POOR
Sylvia Law   28001   1.25

THE RIGHTS OF PRISONERS
David Rudovsky   07591   .95

THE RIGHTS OF SERVICEMEN
Robert S. Rivkin   28019   1.25

THE RIGHTS OF STUDENTS
Alan H. Levine with Eve Carey and Diane Divoky   05776   .95

THE RIGHTS OF SUSPECTS
Oliver Rosengart   28043   1.25

THE RIGHTS OF TEACHERS
David Rubin   25049   1.50

THE RIGHTS OF WOMEN
Susan Deller Ross   27953   1.75

THE RIGHTS OF REPORTERS
Joel M. Gora   21485   1.50

THE RIGHTS OF HOSPITAL PATIENTS
George J. Annas   22459   1.50

THE RIGHTS OF GAY PEOPLE E. Carrington
Boggan, Marilyn G. Haft, Charles Lister, John P. Rupp 24976   1.75

Wherever better paperbacks are sold, or direct from the publisher. Include 25¢ per copy for mailing; allow three weeks for delivery.

Avon Books, Mail Order Dept.,
250 West 55th Street, New York, N.Y. 10019

ACLU 6-76

DISCUS BOOKS
DISTINGUISHED NON-FICTION

A SELECTION OF RECENT TITLES

DRT 5-76

8423